More Than Winning
The Servant-Leader Coach in Contemporary Society

Marty Durden

"Leadership, like coaching, is fighting for the hearts and souls…and getting them to believe in you." —*Eddie Robinson*

Copyright © 2022 by **Marty Durden**

All rights reserved. No part of this publication may be reproduced, distributed or transmitted in any form or by any means, without prior written permission.

More Than Winning: The Servant-Leader Coach in Contemporary Society/ Marty Durden -- 1st ed.

ISBN 979-8-9874312-0-7

"Do unto others as you would have them do unto you."

—LUKE 6:30

CONTENTS

FOREWORD

CHAPTER ONE
THE INFLUENCE OF A COACH 3

CHAPTER TWO
THE CALLING OF A COACH 20

CHAPTER THREE
DEFINING SERVANT LEADERSHIP..30

CHAPTER FOUR
THE MOTIVATIONAL EFFECTS OF SERVANT-LEADERSHIP COACHING 58

CHAPTER FIVE
TEN THOUSAND SHOTS..74

CHAPTER SIX
RESEARCH CONCLUSIONS 80

CHAPTER SEVEN
THE COACH AS A TEACHER 84

CHAPTER EIGHT
OUTSIDE THE LINES 88

REFERENCES

APPENDICES

ABOUT THE AUTHOR

FOREWORD

I was raised in a small town in southwest Georgia. It was an idyllic little town with only one red light. Family was everything in Attapulgus, Georgia. We attended church every Sunday, and one of my Sunday school teachers was a great man I respected immensely named Ed Stewart.

Looking back on those days as an old man now, I realize that Mr. Stewart was a very strong influence on my life. He was a rugged guy with a tender heart who was a U.S. combat veteran in WWII. He taught us many valuable life lessons from the Bible. Maybe the reason I respected him so much was because he truly believed in me. He had the ability to use stories from the scriptures to teach us about Christ in our everyday lives.

One of the most vivid lessons he taught me was about the Christian work ethic. He believed that a Christian should demonstrate his faith by the quality of the work he did. If a person claimed to be a Christian, he/she should do a better job. The Christian should hold himself to a higher standard. This thought I've carried with me my entire life. Mr. Stewart's lesson has formed the basis for the title of this book...*More Than Winning*.

If the title of this book caught your attention, it is likely that your life has been positively influenced by one of your coaches. That was certainly true in the author's life. Coaches possess a unique platform in our society. My view of life was largely assimilated by coaches and teachers who helped shape my thinking. Although the church was a big part of my life, the people that reached me were not ministers—They were coaches.

The author's hope is that this simple book about the influence of coaches will motivate you to coach a little league team, play golf with your granddaughter or to sign up your child to play for a coach who believes in a higher standard than winning. Coaches possess a unique standing of influence in our society that is largely untarnished. The intention of this writing is that you will become a coach who uses the medium of sport to make a difference in some young person's life.

CHAPTER ONE

THE INFLUENCE OF A COACH

"A coach can do more to influence young people in one day than any preacher in America can do in a year."
– Billy Graham

A Big Pair of Shoes

Coaches make a difference in lives. One day many years ago, four boys were visiting a place where young men did not need to go. It was a rough establishment on the outskirts of their South Georgia hometown, a place where good things seldom happened. On this day the weather was very hot, so they stopped for a drink.

A local baseball coach drove up while the boys sat on the bench in the front of this establishment enjoying their drinks. The coach asked the four boys if they would like to play on his summer baseball team. The first young man replied that he was not interested, and the boy sitting next to him said the same. But the third young man said, "I will if he will," gesturing toward his best friend, the fourth young fellow on the end of the bench. Caught off guard, the fourth boy paused before answering. "Well, I would like to," he said, "but I don't have any baseball shoes."

The coach opened the trunk of his car and dug through the equipment it contained, searching until he found a pair of baseball cleats. They were not new, but they were in decent shape. "Well, if these fit, you can have them," said the coach as he handed the shoes to the last young man on the bench. "That is my size," the boy said in amazement as he sat down on the curb to try them on. The cleats fit perfectly, and true to their word, the two young friends rode away with the coach, leaving their two pals sitting on the bench. Little did they know that they would never return to that place on the outskirts of town.

Later that summer, this same young man stood in the batter's box wearing those cleats the coach had given him. With two strikes in the bottom of the last inning and a tied score, he knew a hit would win the game with his best friend, James, on second base. The coach called time out and told the nervous young athlete, "Just relax. The last time he was ahead in the count, he threw a high fastball. That is your pitch. Don't be afraid to swing if he does it again."

Sure enough, the next pitch was a letter high fastball, and the young man launched a line drive into the right-center gap. His team cheered as his friend, James, crossed the plate with the winning run. The home crowd erupted into the spontaneous roar that accompanies a winning walk-off hit. The young man had never experienced anything like that in his life, and he was overwhelmed with the moment of joy. His coach lifted him up and said, "Way to go, Kid." The only thing the young athlete could think of to say was, "Coach, thanks for those shoes."

Many years have come and gone since that day. The first young man who told Coach Raymond Clyatt that he did not want to play eventually died of a drug overdose. The second young man has endured much struggle in his life as a result of his choices. The owner of that dubious place was murdered years later, and where his establishment once stood is now an empty lot filled with weeds. His death remains an unsolved mystery. The third young man who scored the winning run named James remains my best friend for life. The boy who had no cleats is me... and I have coached for five decades trying to follow Coach Clyatt's example.

I have given my best to pay back Coach for those shoes. As coaches do, he devoted his time to young people and never received any pay for it. He called two of us from a tough situation and showed us that there was something better. He was not able to turn us all around, but he batted .500 that day and took two of us from a place that led to nowhere. Coach was a splendid example of what coaching is all about. He gave me more than a pair of cleats—He gave me a big pair of shoes to fill.

The Transformational Coach

Coaches are transformational figures in our sports culture. Coaches have a platform unequaled, according to legendary basketball coach John Wooden who said, "A good coach can change a game, but a great coach can change a life." Leroy Butler (FSU) speaks of his college coach, Bobby Bowden, in reverent terms by saying, "He pretty much saved my life. I don't know what would have happened, because no school wanted to give me a scholarship since I was Prop 48 (academic casualty) in 1986. He was instrumental in helping me become the player I was and the person I am. The guy is amazing. I owe him a lot" (Frenette, 2021).

Heisman winner and NBA star Charlie Ward, along with college coach Mark Richt, speak of Coach Bowden with reverence due to his influence upon their lives. Richt credits Bowden with changing the trajectory of his life. As a result of Coach Bowden's influence, Mark Richt became a Christian.

Charlie Ward's unparalleled career is chronicled in his biography, *The Athlete*. The foundation of his career was laid by the principles he learned from his father, Charlie Ward, Sr., who was a legendary high school coach in Thomasville, GA. Charlie learned many lessons from his father and is himself a high school coach today. He won the Heisman, the NCAA National Championship, was point guard for the New York Knicks and coached in the NBA. He is one of the most amazing athletes in the history of United States sports, yet remains a humble servant-leader coach to high school athletes in Tallahassee. His is the personification of a Christian coach in our contemporary society. Like many of us, Charlie's life was influenced by great coaches, and he is carrying that torch to future generations.

Servant-leader coaches have a lasting impact on their players. The obligation to mentor young men and women is incumbent in the profession of coaching. My guess is that you, the reader, had a coach who made a lasting impact on your life…and that is one reason you are reading this book. As a result of coaches pouring themselves into our lives, we feel compelled to "pay it forward" in the lives of other young people. If you feel this, maybe God is speaking to you.

Coaches possess an innate ability of influence young people in our society. A 2009 study reported in the *Psychology of Sport and Exercise* revealed that "the influence of coaches related most strongly to the manner in which they perform their roles of instruction and assessment" (Keegan, 2009). In this and other studies, the evidence indicates that the coach is a significant influence in the lives of their players. The evidence of this study points to the teaching impact that the coach imparts to players.

When the word *assessment* is mentioned in this study, it pertains to the goals that are developed through the coach-player relationship that guide the team members to reach for improvement in their lives, as well as their improved abilities as players.

Our worth as coaches is to motivate young people to develop a purpose that is guided by goals. This research supports the notion that teaching is a key element in our role as Coach. In my interviews with players, a constant refrain from the young people is that they desire to have a leader who makes them a better player, as well as a better person. Young people seek mentors whom they trust and lean on so that they can improve their lives. The mentor relationship provided by the coach has a lasting imprint on the behavior of players. Young people who strive to give their best effort in practice are usually willing to work with the same intensity to improve the quality of their lives.

The link that enjoins the coach and their players is larger than sports—It motivates the player to strive for higher ideals in their lives… The coach who utilizes his/her influence to gain the trust of young athletes makes one of the most significant and lasting impacts on young people. This is the reason that the coach in our society is respected and transformational. The work that originates in the coach/player trust relationship is the essence of the 'higher standard' that we seek. Servant-leader coaches seek maximum effort on the field and off from their players. The core of coaching is the coach and player working together consistently with the goal to improve athletic skills, as well as their lives. The work is the goal; the wins are the byproduct.

More Than Winning

> *"Success is the peace of mind that comes as a direct result of the satisfaction in knowing that you are doing all you can do to be the best that you are capable of becoming."*
>
> – John Wooden

Winners do not emphasize wins.

The Higher Standard principle is more than emphasis on winning. All coaches want to win, but to emphasize winning above all else is measuring success by a false societal standard. The player or coach who dwells on winning will endure much frustration. As Dean Smith once said, "If everything about your coaching is life or death, you will die a lot." Seeking a higher standard is about *succeeding* rather than winning.

John Wooden is the most successful NCAA men's basketball coach in history, based on an unprecedented .808 winning percentage, induction into the Basketball Hall of Fame as both a player and coach, and ten NCAA men's basketball national titles. With the many accolades that have accompanied the success of John Wooden's basketball coaching career, you will not find a player who ever heard him utter the words "win" or "lose." Wooden judged success by a higher standard than wins. His definition of success is "the peace of mind that comes as a direct result in knowing that you did all you could to become the best that you are capable of becoming." He believed that you cannot ask a player to give more than he or she is capable of, but you can certainly expect every player to give their best effort.

John Wooden's philosophy of coaching is a good study for our profession. His unique coaching techniques distinguish his career. Wooden considered himself principally a teacher rather than a coach. He believed that the coach is nothing more than a teacher, and his sport is the classroom. One of Wooden's most widely known teaching methods was his development of the Pyramid of Success, which we see in coaches' offices across the country.

Interestingly, the concept of the Pyramid of Success did not originate from his coaching, but rather from his English classroom. One day a parent asked Coach Wooden about his son's English grade and expressed his dismay that he had received a C rather than an A. Wooden realized that the student was doing his best in the class and counseled the father that it is unfair to demand more than his son was capable of giving. Wooden viewed this as an unreasonable expectation that was counter-productive to the success of this young man. The Pyramid of Success that is largely associated with the accolades of John Wooden's coaching career was intended to help parents of students in his English class to set realistic expectations for their final grade. Wooden rightfully believed that he is a teacher first and a coach second. The basketball court is merely his classroom.

The Pyramid of Success is a framework of behaviors that originated in the teaching of Wooden's father. Wooden spent decades identifying the characteristics and traits that help define a successful person and narrowed the list to 25 common behaviors. By 1948, he created the iconic triangular diagram and named it the "Pyramid of Success." This model provides an accurate rudder guiding the true purpose of our efforts as coaches.

In the competitive world of athletics, it is easy for a coach to get lost in the pursuit of winning and forget the reason we followed the call to coach. Success in our profession cannot be measured in a winning percentage or the display of titles in our trophy case. Building deep and abiding relationships is the goal of our calling. These relationships will make a difference in many lives, including our own. My advice to every young coach is to study the teaching methods and philosophy of John Wooden. His Pyramid is a perfect model of the principles that embody the Higher Standard.

*The Pyramid of Success can be found in Appendix A in this publication.

When winning alone dominates our coaching philosophy, the joy that comes from participating is minimized. The goal of sports is to enjoy the competition and to grow as people. One story that I witnessed provides a perfect example of why we play the game. We were playing a critical football game on a cold wintry night. One of our running backs was a player named Travis Hargrove, who remains one of my dearest friends. Travis played great that night despite the rough conditions. The game was played on one of those frigid winter nights with sleet falling from a windy sky. Field conditions were horrible, and neither team was able to move the ball easily. It was a muddy slugfest, and in the fourth quarter, our opponent was able to score the winning touchdown. We gave it all we had that night but came up short on the scoreboard.

As we trudged up the hill to our dressing room, I walked beside Travis quietly. He was our leading rusher and played a good game. The sleet was falling on us. Travis was covered in mud and sweat with some blood on his uniform. The steam was rising from his uniform as we took our solemn walk when suddenly my young son, Tyler, appeared. He grabbed Travis' hand and walked with us. He looked up to Travis and said, "You played awesome!" Travis replied with a smile, "Thank you, Tyler." Then Tyler spoke these amazing words: "Who won?" Travis and I looked at each other and smiled. Tyler loved Travis unconditionally—His admiration for his friend did not factor in the score. We finished our walk to the dressing room, but our steps were lighter knowing that we cannot completely judge our success on scoreboards—Tyler reminded us of a higher standard than winning.

Everyone needs a person in their life to remind them of their core principles. My son, Tyler, has always been that person to me. His beliefs are unshakable, and he lives his principles. He is not a man of many words, but his actions speak volumes. He has encouraged me to write this book and supports my career in coaching. The demands of the call have often been at the expense of my family. The regrets that exist in my life center around the guilt that comes from not giving my family enough of my time. My suggestion to all coaches is to make sure that you do not neglect the needs of your spouse and children. This is the biggest challenge in the profession—finding time for what matters. Every coach needs a son like Tyler, who reminds them of the person that we need to be by his example. He has that quiet strength that I admire. Sometimes we coaches talk too much and do not walk enough. Our example speaks volumes— This is what I am learning in my life and is attributed to the example of my son, Tyler.

Servant-leader coaches spend their time in the process rather than the product. Winning is a byproduct of good coaching, rather than the sole purpose of coaching. Judging our success as coaches by a win/loss record is misleading. We should not be concerned about things we cannot control, but we *can* control our inputs...our attitude, our effort, our work ethic. We cannot control the weather, the bounce of the ball, the motivation of our opponents, the result of officials' rulings, the rub of the green or the ups and downs of our competitors. Smart coaches realize that they need to live in the present and keep focus on the things that are within their power to control.

Coaching from the inside-out is the principle of prioritizing our input into the character of our players. Nick Saban, the head football coach at the University of Alabama, describes this as focusing on the person and not the outcome. He believes, "The process is about staying in the present and laying siege to the obstacle in front of you. It is about not getting distracted by anything else that comes your way." By staying in the process of working to become the best we can be, we are focused on the "precious present." The coach who allows his team to become focused on outcomes is shortchanging the path that leads to success.

One of Saban's most revealing principles is: "Don't think about winning the SEC Championship. Don't think about the

National Championship. Think about what you needed to do in this drill, on this play, in this moment. That's the process. Let's think about what we can do today in the task at hand."

Leaders should motivate teams to live in the present and prevent players from drifting away off the path that leads to success. By staying focused, we maximize the chance to be successful. The road to success is built on the foundation of work. The servant-leader coach needs to emphasize this concept of staying in the process. Enjoy the journey... It leads to the destination. Follow the path, and do not be distracted. We must focus on the things that we can control. Success is not found in wins and losses, but rather the work we contribute to become the best we are capable of being. The journey to success is much more important than the destination. Bill Russell, one of the greatest winners of all time, once said, "We work to become, not to acquire." The process is what makes us better, not the outcome.

> *"The only place where you can find success before work is in the dictionary."*
>
> — Anonymous

Work

Central to the process is hard work. Good coaching principles place the work ethic in the middle of team culture. The accountability of each team member to do their best is integral to improvement. Players who work side-by-side to accomplish their goals and hold each other accountable create an environment that drives everyone to give their best. While we cannot control some things, we can control our inputs—We are solely responsible for our work. My advice to players is that if you want to earn respect from others, you earn it by your work. Successful teams work side-by-side. One phrase I love in the FCA Competitor's Creed is, "My sweat is an offering." The contribution one should make to the team culture is hard work evidenced by sweat equity.

If you desire to be respected by others, you gain that by hard work. The culture of successful teams is built on effort. Three things help to build a culture that promotes success: (1) Complete effort daily, (2) Being a good teammate, (3) Tracking your improvement. Players who strive to accomplish these three things each day, become the standard for other players to emulate. Team leaders emerge within the culture by exhibiting these three qualities—They earn the referent power to be leaders because others respect their hard work. The player who only offers words does not gain the trust of the team. Player leadership is displayed by the example of consistent hard work.

The culture of sports can be described as a meritocracy. Coaches cannot afford to give favors to players; everything on the team must be earned. In the interviews with athletes during my research, this statement is often spoken by players and discussed in small groups. High school athletes base much of their coach's trustworthiness by the way he/she awards playing time to teammates. Team culture centers on trust. Each member of the team trusts their teammates to give their best effort in practice and to carry their load of the work required to make the team function efficiently.

Bear Bryant once said, "It is not the will to win that matters—Everyone has that. It is the will to *prepare* to win that matters." Everyone wants to win. America loves a winner. Not everyone has the will to pay the price that winning requires. Preparation is the duty of the coach—making sure that practices are focused, intense and organized. A study conducted in Florida identified the attributes of their coach that motivated them to give their sustained effort even when confronted with adversity. Seventeen traits were identified in the sample study, and 4,200 Florida athletes selected the traits that motivated them the most.

Their number one pick was an organized, intense, and focused practice. The last factor on the list that these athletes selected was the coach's win-loss record. The study indicated that players want a good practice from the coach and value the coach's accolades very little.

Following closely behind the number one motivator was a coach who played the best players based on fairness. The players believe that organized work is the answer to winning. The study cited an efficient, focused practice as the key to their success—That is what our players said they need in their poll. Our players place far less value on our past exploits than what we can provide to them in the form of expertise, organization, feedback and instruction.

"Success is not owned—it is leased. And the rent is due every day."

—JJ Watt

Virtuous Coaching

In 2020, Lyman Ellis conducted a study entitled: *Do Coaches Who Are Servant Leaders Promote Virtue in Their Athletes?* The study surveyed 274 collegiate soccer players seeking to determine if servant-leadership coaching improved competitive behaviors. The conclusion of the study linked positive servant-leader coaching to improved sportsmanship. "Correlational analyses suggest that when athletes perceive their coaches as servant leaders, athletes tend to show respect for rules and officials, and show concern for opponents. When athletes perceive their coaches as servant leaders, incidences of unsportsmanlike behavior on the field, as reflected in yellow and red card team aggregates, tend to diminish (Ellis, 2020). The example of the coach affects the behavior of the team. An older coach told me that if you (the coach) do not stay poised, how can you expect your players to?

Once I witnessed a junior high basketball game. It was a close game with numerous ups and downs. One coach was calm and poised, while the other was fraught with emotional outbursts directed toward both players and officials. The score was tied with a few seconds remaining when two of the opponents were battling for a loose ball. The official blew his whistle and called a foul on one of the girls on the team, awarding a free throw with only one second remaining on the clock. The young player who committed the foul was devastated and in tears. Her coach called timeout, came across the floor and hugged the player. Her teammates surrounded her with support. It was evident that her coach was focused on *her* and not worried about the outcome of her foul. She demonstrated unconditional love and support for her player while ignoring the outcome of the game. It was evident by her actions that she cared more about her team than the final score.

The young lady missed the foul shot, and the game went into overtime. The game continued for three extra minutes when, with ten seconds remaining, a player on the other team fouled the same young lady who had committed the foul prior. The coach of the offending player poured her anger at the young player, as well as the official who called the foul. The coach made no attempt to huddle with her team while the other team was eagerly listening to their coach. Rather than huddling, the irate coach paced down the sideline protesting the call and ventilating her anger. When the huddle broke, the last words of the positive coach was, "Give it all you have!" The young player calmly walked to the free throw line and sank both shots.

Never have I witnessed a more poignant example of how a coach's influence makes a difference. The example of this coach during the crucible of athletic competition is more important than any spoken words. Reassurance from a coach rather than public scolding is an affirmation that fills the emotional tanks of our players. Kids feel terrible about game mistakes—The coach only makes this worse with reprimands and outbursts. Our players need to feel that we are confident and believe in them. Mistakes are inherent in sports, and helping players overcome them is part of servant-leadership.

An additional study performed by G. Matthew Robinson and Marshall J. Magnusen in November 2020 entitled *Servant Leadership, Leader Effectiveness, and the Role of Political Skill: A Study of Interscholastic Sport Administrators* revealed, "Servant leadership is directly related to leader effectiveness, effective organizational commitment, and job satisfaction of head coaches" (Robinson, 2022). Research validates a more positive team culture and higher levels of motivation resulting from servant-leadership coaching constructs.

The example of the coach who lives by the rules of conduct that he subscribes magnifies his influence. The coach who demonstrates genuine concern to players has much more motivational influence on behaviors than the coach who dwells on results. Players follow the coach that does what she says, whose actions back her words.

"If a man does his best, what else is there?"

—General George S. Patton

Praying to Win

Many of my coaching colleagues admit that they pray for their team to win. This is a debate among coaches…Is it right to pray for a win? My view is that God expects us to do our best. I Corinthians 9:24 states, "Do you not know that in a race all the runners run, but only one gets the prize? Run in such a way as to get the prize." God believes it is okay to try to win, but I doubt that He really cares who wins. He cares about us—not about our record. Coaches can easily get confused about accomplishments and lose track of the primary purpose of coaching.

When I was a young basketball coach, my dear Aunt Lou asked my wife, Diane, and me to come for supper. During the meal, she asked me, "How have you been doing?" I responded, "Right now we are 6 and 4." Diane whispered, "I think she means, how are YOU doing, not your team's record." So, I responded, "Well, other than that we are pretty good."

My response was a lame attempt to redirect the conversation. God expects us to do our best regardless of a win-loss record. In fact, our efforts should be directed in another way rather than the applause of others. Colossians 3:23 states, "Whatever you do, work heartily, as for the Lord and not for men."

The approval of God is what the Christian coach in contemporary society should seek. Minimizing the desire to win is not what this author is attempting to do in this writing. In fact, professional successes do lend a deep sense of fulfillment and create value in our vocation. Winning coaches have more opportunities to influence others. Striving to win is expected in our society and provides a strong motivation for the organization to work. However, placing *all* our emphasis on wins becomes the problem. The principle of keeping our eyes on the goal is crucial in both sports and our pursuit of the call. An appropriate passage to reflect this principle is Hebrews 12:1-2.

> *"Therefore, since we are surrounded by such a great cloud of witnesses, let us throw off everything that hinders and the sin that so easily entangles. And let us run with perseverance the race marked out for us, fixing our eyes on Jesus, the pioneer and perfecter of faith. For the joy set before him he endured the cross, scorning its shame, and sat down at the right hand of the throne of God."*

The Christian coach's goal is to do our best for someone else's glory—not our egos. This is the tightrope that we walk in our lives: trying to win, but doing it with the correct motive. Every day of my life, I should give all my effort to do my best—just as Mr. Stewart taught in Sunday school decades ago. That is why our call is to a higher standard than winning. When our efforts are for applause of the public, we are settling for less than the Higher Standard. *More than winning* is what we should seek. Accolades can become a dangerous drug in our lives if we allow the desire for popularity to consume us.

Popularity is temporary. When Jesus entered Jerusalem on Palm Sunday, thousands of people lined the streets and cheered, laying palms for Him to tread. He was greeted as a popular hero. In less than a week he was crucified on a cross and hung between two thieves. As coach Dan Henning once said, "Popularity is somewhere between Palm Sunday and Good Friday." The praise we seek is from an audience of one.

My perspective on being a career coach is that too much emphasis on winning will not lead to fulfillment. If winning is all a coach pursues, he cannot win enough to feed that thirst. We all love to win, and we all strive to win. Our goal as coaches is to win championships for the team, and we cannot escape the fact that our livelihood (professional coaches) often depends on results. Winning provides a degree of satisfaction, but what sustains us as coaches is more than what winning can provide. What we remember most and what fuels our drive is the relationships that we make in this field of competition that we call sports. The competition that we enter together is the crucible that forges the deep relationships that last throughout our lifetime. Battling side-by-side is the bond that enjoins us and builds the camaraderie unique to sports.

Before you pray for your team to win, remember this quote from Yogi Berra. He was catching a game in Yankee Stadium before a cheering crowd when an opposing batter approached the plate uttering a prayer for success. Before he entered the batter's box he drew a cross in the dirt, crossed himself and looked toward heaven. Yogi's advice to him was, "Why don't you leave God alone and let Him enjoy the game." My epitaph will not have my win-loss record as I responded to Aunt Lou. Hope the words are – "Well done, my good and faithful servant."

My belief is that God does not care who wins, but he cares about me.

CHAPTER TWO

THE CALLING OF A COACH

"The two greatest days of your life are the day you were born, and the day you find out why you were born."
– Lou Holtz

Coaching is a calling. There is a difference in primary calling and our vocational calling. Our primary calling is to establish a personal relationship with Christ. An avocation is a hobby, or any other activity taken up in addition to one's regular work; it may especially refer to something that is a person's true passion or interest. A *vocation* is one's principal occupation and their source of income. *Calling* is often used in the context of a calling to a particular way of life or course of action, such as being a pastor. Many people have a passion for sports such as golfers, fisherman, tennis players or lay coaches. Their avocation may or may not be a source of income…it is something they do that lends meaning to their lives. Thus, we can have a vocational call, as well as an avocational call.

The best-case scenario is that the vocational call and avocational call are the same. In my life, this has been true. Millions of coaches in our country are truly bi-vocational. Coach Clyatt's vocation was as a freight agent for Seaboard Coastline Railroad, but his avocational calling as a lay coach made a difference in the lives of many young people in my hometown. As a result of his avocation, I followed in his and other coaches' footsteps and am a coach today. Quite possibly, God could call any of us to do two things. The Apostle Paul was a tent maker by vocation, but one of the principal biblical authors and pioneers in the early church. The principal calling in your life could very possibly have two different faces. As you seek God's guidance in your life, remember that many coaches wear two hats. Our savior, Jesus Christ was a carpenter, but His primary purpose was to die on the cross to save us from our sins. The legacy of our avocation often supersedes our vocational accomplishments and lends more fulfillment.

In the United States, the number of volunteer coaches is estimated between 3.5 and 6 million people. The majority of these are not professional coaches, but rather people who feel that by coaching they can make a difference in the lives of young people. These are not motivated by tangible rewards—They seek to be positive influences. My belief is that these volunteers were influenced by a coach at some point in their lives and are trying to make this same contribution to a young person as a token of their gratitude. They are "passing the baton."

One objective of this writing is to help these volunteer coaches become effective mentors and equip them in this task as we seek to understand the depth of importance that coaching holds in the lives of others. This desire to pass the baton is the essence of the calling that motivates coaches. The purpose of this author is to affirm the call to coach and to inform all coaches, both professional and volunteer, about the transformational power of servant-leader coaching. Many coaches have a "Coach Clyatt" in their lives—a person that may have changed the trajectory of their journey. My desire is to affirm the tremendous motivational power that servant-leadership coaching provides. The servant-leader coach follows a higher calling seeking more than winning—He or she pursues a Higher Standard than winning.

These coaches lead youth teams throughout our nation with an estimated 60 million participants aged six to eighteen. The potential to influence these young people is staggering. If coaches simply personify the principles of servant-leading, the impact of this philosophy will be multiplied for generations. The transformational power of servant-leadership coaching will change the complexion of our culture. The call for virtuous coaches has never been more critical.

In the 2022 FCA camp video message, great words from coach Bobby Bowden were expressed that, "Coaching is a calling. When we are called to coach, we have a responsibility to take care of those under our care." The call is not something to take casually, but rather constitutes an important aspect of influence. Servant-leaders are purposed to lead from the heart and to help others become the best that they can become. James, the brother of Christ, advises (in James 3:1-2) that following the leadership call means that coaches will be judged by a higher standard. Therefore, before following this call, we should consider the weight of responsibility that it involves.

Not everyone is called to coach, but those who are will be "judged by a stricter standard." This fact is what Coach Bowden alluded to when he said that we hold a responsibility to develop the young people under our care.

God calls all Christians to serve, but many simply refuse to follow through and answer. These words are appropriate today in our modern culture. Many Christians prefer to occupy a comfortable pew on Sunday mornings rather than to answer the call to serve in their daily lives. Not everyone is called to coach, but we are invited to follow Christ by helping others. The heart of servant-leading is to find a spot where you see a need and answer the call. Answering the call involves self-examination to discover where our gifts and talents lie. Before God calls us to serve, He will equip us.

One of the primary considerations in this "stricter standard" is the fact that young people are constantly watching us. My mother always said, "You can fool adults, but children see through your charade." I ran across this poem decades ago in a publication, and these words explain mom's wisdom.

> There are little eyes upon you, and they're watching night and day,
> There are little ears that quickly take in every word you say,
> There are little hands all eager to do anything you do,
> And a little boy who's dreaming of the day he'll be like you.
> You're the little fellow's idol
> You're the wisest of the wise,
> In his little mind about you no suspicions ever rise,
> He believes in you devoutly, holds that all you say and do,
> He will say and do like you do in your way
> When he's grown up just like you.
> There's a wide-eyed little fellow who believes you're always right,
> And his ears are always open and he watches day and night.
> You are setting an example every day in all you do,
> For the little boy who's waiting to grow up to be like you.

I was blessed to coach a young man named Andre Taylor. When Andre was a very young child, his parents abandoned him and left him on the doorstep of their neighbor's house. He was raised by a family that loved him as one of their own, but he had no biological father in his life. When I met Andre, he was a sophomore. He impressed me with his work ethic and attitude. He was the consummate team player and was blessed with athletic ability. Andre was one of those special players who made me a better coach. He had a positive effect on everyone around him.

We were lucky to have a very talented basketball team, and it was difficult to narrow our roster to only twelve players. Andre was a good player who could make almost any roster in our state, but we were not able to keep him on the roster because of our deep talent pool. The day after we cut him, Andre asked me if he could still come to practice and help us. We made him the student assistant coach.

He was an incredible asset to the team and was obviously talented as a coach. Late that season our team was affected by influenza, and we only had seven players available against the number one ranked team in the state. So, we asked Andre to dress and play. Against the best team in the state, Andre scored 12 points, got 10 rebounds, and played like a champion. We were not able to beat them that night, but we were competitive and "gave them all they wanted." I was so proud of him. He thanked us for letting him play. How many young men do you know who would do something like that? It was one of those moments in my profession that I am glad God called me. At this point in my life, I began to see that God's leading in Andre's life was moving him in the same direction as me. In my heart, I began to see that Andre would make a good coach.

Back in those days, an evangelistic group of athletes named The Power Team came to our town. The Power Team was a group of extremely strong men who preached to young people. Their feats of strength were incredible. They could rip phone books, break out of handcuffs, bend steel bars...unbelievable feats. I invited six of the guys from our weight training program to attend the Power Team event in a stadium. The six guys were Andre, Eric, Dexter, Otis, Donnell and Alfred. All were good athletes and loved to lift weights. We went to see The Power Team, along with thousands of other students and coaches. Their evangelistic message was very strong, and they gave an invitation when finished.

Some of our guys went down and were even baptized on the field with a large group of young people from other schools. It was an exciting event. Otis was one of the guys who was baptized, and about a month later he was killed in a car accident. Dexter was also baptized. He was a great basketball player who signed a scholarship to play.

I remember him talking about his baptism weeks later when Otis was killed. Dexter's words were, "I am glad Otis walked down to be baptized that night. When I saw him get up, I followed him. I would not have gone if Otis did not." When I received word years later that Dexter was killed in an accident, I remembered that night. If we had not gone to that event years ago, just think how differently their lives could have ended. They went because their coach asked them to go.

My admonition to coaches is to get into the lives of your players and know them. If you sincerely care about your team, they will respect you. Sometimes we only see the present—this game, this practice, this event—but we need to be mindful of the permanent consequences of our relationships with our players. Someone asked Joe Ehrmann this question: "Coach, how is your team?" His answer was, "I don't know yet...ask me again in twenty years." Coaches have a tremendous influence on their team. Of these six guys, Andre is a coach, Donnell a preacher, Alfred and Eric have become great adults who are making a difference in lives.

When Andre was a college student, he called me on the phone one afternoon and asked these words: "Coach, do you think I could be a coach?" My answer was, "Andre, I think you were born to be a coach. You would be an ideal coach and will be much better than me. A few years later, he called again with these words: "Coach, I just got hired to be a basketball coach, and you are the first person I thought should know." I was overjoyed, and it honestly was one of the happiest moments I can remember. Just two years ago, Andre was named Coach-of-the-Year in the entire state of Georgia—not a bad accomplishment for a guy who was left on a doorstep. He remains one of the best basketball coaches in our state.

The story of Andre Taylor's call to coach is an amazing episode of how coaches find their niche. Simply witnessing his life and how he became a coach is one of the most rewarding stories I have seen. I am honored to know Andre, and he has made me a much better person. His story is one of the reasons why it is difficult to explain the call. Everyone has a different story about how God led them to find their place.

Answering the Call

One of the biggest influences in my life is Dr. Chip Reese. Among the many talents he possesses is that he is an amazing baseball coach. Years ago, he left the profession and in due time began to miss it. He struggled about the decision to return, and like many of us, could not seem to find a way back. Chip and I were good friends, but during his struggle, our friendship deepened. He is a very talented coach, and during that period of struggle in his life, we were able to coach a young school baseball team together.

Not only did we have a great deal of fun together, but he taught me many of the intricacies of a game he loved dearly. Maybe it was coaching this youth team that Chip began to see just how much he missed coaching. Chip was an expert coach and was overly qualified for many of the jobs he considered. This was a difficult period in his life, and I was honored to be there with him. But, he just could not find a coaching job no matter how much he tried.

Then one night, he dropped by the house. He told Diane and me that he began to realize that maybe God's purpose for his life did not include coaching. It seemed like every time a coaching job looked promising, it just vanished. Chip said this: "I want to coach, but if God does not want that for me, then <u>I am willing</u> to do anything He leads." The statement impacted me deeply, because I knew how much he wanted to coach again. His willingness really struck a chord in my heart...and evidently in God's heart, because the phone rang about ten minutes after Chip left with those words "I am willing" still ringing in my ears.

Ironically, my oldest son is Chip Durden, who was playing baseball at a nearby junior college. Chip Durden's words on the phone were, "Dad, you are not going to believe what I am about to tell you. We just heard our coach is leaving. Do you think Coach Reese would be interested in coaching here?" I could not believe it, and I told my son, "I am pretty sure he will be interested." I hung up with Chip Durden and immediately called Chip Reese. "Would you be interested in coaching at the college?" Chip Reese answered, "I would."

I was so excited that I hung up without saying goodbye, I called the athletic director at the college and discovered that they already had him as the first name on their list of potential candidates. Within 24 hours he was interviewed and before the week ended was announced as the new head coach. His career has flourished since that day...after he said, "I am willing." The timing of Chip's call was incredible. After the words "I am willing," it was less than ten minutes. That fact cannot be ignored.

Every coach has a different story about their call. It is difficult to explain how God calls us, but I believe strongly that He finds people who are willing. Both Andre and Chip Reese make me proud that God called us. John Wooden's first book was entitled *They Call Me Coach*.

I seriously considered titling this book *God Called Me to Coach*.

The Call for a Higher Standard

In recent years, many schools have sullied their reputations by allowing unscrupulous coaches to lay aside their ethics in the pursuit of winning athletic contests on the backs of young athletes. The irony of this is that many of these wrongdoers, after being dismissed, have been rehired by other institutions. We have witnessed the damage done by NCAA basketball coaches offering bribes, college trainers who prey on female athletes, FIFA officials who solicit kickbacks and professional athletes who use performance enhancing drugs. Ethical leaders are dismayed at the negative impact this brings to our profession.

I propose a remedy to this ethical crisis. Let us hire coaches who pursue a higher standard than winning. We need sports leaders, athletic directors, college presidents, high school principals and school administrators to seek servant-leaders as coaches in their schools. To counterbalance these scandals, the world of sports needs coaches who operate by a higher standard than winning alone provides. Servant-leader coaches seek to make a positive difference in lives that serves to honor their calling as leaders.

Servant-leader coaches operate on the foundation of trust that originates in their competency as coaches, their affection for their players, the worth they bestow in the lives of their players and the sense of fairness that governs their decisions. While the servant-leader coach develops teams to win games, they pursue more consequential results than wins or losses. The servant-leader coach lives in the process and values this more than outcomes. Winning games becomes the byproduct of their mission rather than the sole aim.

Coaching from the inside-out develops young people who are prepared for the challenges of life twenty years down the road.

The Higher Standard Coach avoids coercion and prefers to motivate their players as constructive mentors. Young people today are averse to authoritarian leadership principles and prefer coaches who seek to develop them as both people and athletes. My research has shown that servant-leadership coaching elicits a higher level of sustained effort. Young people who view their coach through the lens of trust tend to face the crucible of athletics with a higher degree of determination.

My proposition is that we have reached the critical point in our sports culture where we need to issue the call for coaches who pursue a higher standard than winning. The Higher Standard is the antidote to the incipient uptick of unethical incidents in our beloved profession.

Coaching involves more than just winning.

CHAPTER THREE

DEFINING SERVANT LEADERSHIP

*"Life's most persistent and urgent question is,
'What are you doing for others?"*
– Dr. Martin Luther King, Jr.

Servant-leaders emphasize people above product. Servant-leadership differs from traditional forms of leadership because of the value placed upon the people within the organization. Kathleen Patterson describes servant-leadership as "follower focus" (Patterson, 2008). Robert K. Greenleaf stresses the "care taken by the servant first to make sure that other people's highest priority needs are being served" (Greenleaf, 2008).

Established leadership styles place high emphasis upon hierarchal models whereby power flows from the top down. Servant-leadership flips the customary leadership model by leading from the bottom-up. This type of leadership is sometimes referred to as inverted leadership. The counter-cultural model is based upon follower input that creates an innovative atmosphere of mutual ownership. Follower input characterizes servant-leaders who validate followers and is an idea that has gained momentum in recent years. It is employed by many successful corporations, schools, and faith-based organizations.

Servant-leadership is growing in popularity and has enjoyed widespread acceptance regarding the value of this methodology. Servant-leadership has been compared and contrasted to transformational leadership. Kathleen B. Patterson posits that the leader leads "with a heart to serve" and by "truly loving your followers...doing the right things for people...." (Patterson, 2003).

Greenleaf believes the "difference manifests itself in the care taken by the servant, first to make sure that other people's highest priority needs are being served" (Greenleaf, 1970). Kristen Galek states that leadership starts on the inside. "An individual acts on his/her heart. Their core vision and values drive their motivation and intentions as a servant-leader" (Galek, 2015).

Greenleaf's teachings repositioned the seemingly paradoxical terms of *servant* and *leader*. In the majority of authority models, the leader is placed first and the follower last. Servant-leadership's counter-cultural teachings reversed these contradictory concepts. Combining servant and leader into a dyad created a new paradigm of leadership theory, and many distinguished leaders have adopted the premise of servant-leadership. Some of these leaders are Ken Blanchard, Jim Blanchard, Max DePree, M. Scott Peck, Bill Turner, Stephen Covey, Larraine Matusak, and Steve Butler (Spears, 2010). One of the strongest endorsements of the value of servant-leadership comes from Danah Zohar (1979) who states, "Servant-leadership is the essence of quantum thinking and leadership" (Zohar, 1979).

Many of these seminal ideas were published in an essay written by Greenleaf entitled *The Servant as Leader*, first published in 1970. When Greenleaf was an executive at AT&T, he became interested in the notion of the leader as a servant. His ideas were generated from his reading of a book authored by Herman Hesse (*Journey to the East*) describing a fictitious character who exemplified the traits of servant-leadership (Spears, 2008).

Greenleaf has since founded the Greenleaf Center for Servant-Leadership, which serves as one principal source of information on this topic. The center sponsors programs, seminars, and web-based sites to enlighten interested parties about the value of servant-leadership.

The irony of leadership is that before we can be leaders, we must be followers. The call of Jesus is simply, "Follow Me." Following the principles of leadership that Jesus employed is the essence of servant-leadership. While leading and serving seem to be opposing concepts, servant-leadership differs from traditional forms of leadership because of the value placed upon the people within the organization.

The servant-leader coach emphasizes people rather than product. The authoritarian coach that existed for decades in our society is being replaced by the coach who stresses relationships above coercion, including their ideas in the decision-making process. The ultimate gauge of effective servant-leaders is not how many followers they have, but how many leaders they have produced.

Peter G. Northouse defines servant-leadership as a "paradox" that seems to be a contradiction of "common sense" (Northouse, 2013). Northouse stresses that servant-leadership is exhibited in the leader's behaviors rather than as a trait of the leadership philosophy (Northouse, 2013). Serving and leading simultaneously does defy the conventional logic of leadership. Serving denotes submission, while leading suggests authority. The paradoxical linking of two seemingly contradictory terms--serving and leading--is the essence of servant-leadership.

Robert K. Greenleaf is one of the most prolific authors presenting the virtues of servant-leading. His basic premise teaches that the "servant-leader is a servant first." Greenleaf values serving above power and giving rather than receiving (Greenleaf, 1977/2002). His ten characteristics of servant-leadership are:

listening, empathy, healing, awareness, persuasion, conceptualization, foresight, stewardship, commitment to the growth of people, and building community (Spears, 2010).

Greenleaf is credited with creating the term "servant-leadership" in 1970, and his teachings represented a shift from the hierarchical models of authoritative leadership. The ten basic characteristics that he espoused provide the framework of this philosophy. He believes that including others in decision-making demonstrates an inherent worth in their input. Authentic, empathetic listening followed by reflection validates the importance of other people (Spears, 2009).

Servant-leadership is about people.

The Scriptural Origin of Servant-Leadership

> *"Let nothing be done through selfish ambition or conceit, but in lowliness of mind let each esteem others better than himself. Let each of you look out not only for his own interests, but also for the interests of others."*
>
> – Philippians 2:3-4

Servant-leadership is a topic that is widely discussed in the business field and generally accepted as an efficient leadership theory. Corporate leaders continually search for methods to motivate employees, attempting to increase efficiency and maximize profits. Servant-leadership is a philosophy that works for many business leaders.

Even though Robert Greenleaf is often referred to as the "father of servant-leadership," as he was the first to coin the words servant-leadership, the philosophy itself originated in the teachings of Christ. Christ repeatedly used the word *servant* in his teachings on leading. In Mark 9:35, we read, "*Sitting down, Jesus called the Twelve and said, 'Anyone who wants to be first must be the very last, and the servant of all.'*" The first coupling of leading and serving originated in the teachings of Christ.

Servant-leadership is an ancient philosophy that still resonates effectively in our modern world. The timeless concepts of the "Golden Rule" constitute the core of this philosophy. "*Do unto others as you would have them do unto you.*" The concept of servant-leadership is rooted in this very simple principle found in ancient biblical scriptures.

Jesus once taught His disciples the value of humility, as described in the parable written in Matthew 20:1-16. In this scripture, Jesus said to his disciples the familiar words, "*So the last will be first, and the first will be last*" (NAS Bible, 1995). He added in this parable: "*Whoever wants to become great among you must be your servant, and whoever wants to be first must be your slave*" (NAS, 1995).

Christ personified servant-leadership throughout His ministry on earth. His leadership opposed coercion. Instead He exemplified humility as He washed the feet of His followers on the night before His arrest (John 13:1-20). He never sought a title or held an office. He forgave His persecutors upon the cross as He was dying (Luke 23:34). My view is that Jesus was the originator and first practitioner of servant-leadership. His life was a life of service and humility that purveyed the historical origin of servant-leadership. Even though He is God, He chose to take the form of a servant to establish His example of leadership. Jesus Christ chose to be a servant as His preferred model for leadership (NAS Bible, 1995). Thus the origin of servant-leadership can be found in the life of Christ as written in the Holy Bible.

Many other ancient references exist that also refer to this style of leadership throughout history. Plato, Aristotle, Socrates,

Confucius, Plutarch, and other renowned philosophers mention the ideals often associated with virtuous leadership. Humility, morality, wisdom, temperance, ethical behavior, and other ideals of leadership are cited in ancient writings such as *Plato's Republic*. History is replete with philosophers and kings who demonstrated humility and anti-authoritarian characteristics. However, no citations linking the words leadership and serving exist in ancient writings.

Not until the teachings of Jesus Christ were these paradoxical meanings combined into a unified theory (NASV Bible, 1995). Servant-leadership is a dyad unique to the teachings of Jesus Christ and establishes the historical origins of the theory of servant-leadership.

If you want to know more about servant-leadership, read about Jesus.

Emergence of the Modern Theory of Servant-Leadership

As a result of writings by Greenleaf and associated servant-leadership theorists, this ancient philosophy has enjoyed a reformation. One study cited in the *Journal of Industrial Psychology* finds that, "Servant-leadership fosters team effectiveness if employees feel committed to their work team" (Mahembe, Engelbrecht, 2014). A study performed by Michelle Vondey (2010) provided "evidence for the relationship between servant-leadership and organizational citizenship behaviors…. (Vondey, 2014).

A recent study in South Africa concluded that a significant positive relationship exists between servant-leadership and trust (Chatbury, 2011). During the investigation of the Penn State football scandal, an article emerged calling for the inclusion of servant-leadership in collegiate athletics (Burton, Peachey, 2013). The article cited the sordid acts perpetrated by Penn State Coach Jerry Sandusky and included other unethical instances that sullied the reputation of collegiate athletics. Burton and Peachey issued a call for ethical leadership as the antidote to these examples of dishonorable actions. This writing expressed the need to consider servant-leadership as a "viable methodology to be studied and supported within the domain of intercollegiate athletics" (Burton, Peachey).

Their writing supported the notion that servant-leadership contains the central component of developing the student-athlete and aligns perfectly with the stated mission of the NCAA. Burton and Peachey admonished sports leaders to re-evaluate the current style of leadership practiced in intercollegiate athletics (Burton, Peachey, 2013).

Modern coaches are discovering that the young players of today accept the tenets of servant-leadership. Today's athlete is different from years past. The much-publicized Generation Y student-athletes (1980's-1995) have moved through college. Generation Y members are often called Millennials. Generation Z is presently being recruited to college, are members of high school teams, and number 23 million. These young people are easily bored, are socially connected to their peers, proficient in technology, and desire to be challenged by their teachers.

Much about this group remains unknown and will emerge as their generation enters adulthood. Generation Z athletes are commonly referred to as Zoomers. Researchers believe Zoomers were born from the mid to late 1990s until 2010. Most members of Generation Z are children of Generation X. Generation Z is the first generation to have grown up with access to the internet and portable digital technology. Members of Generation Z are often called "digital natives."

The seven living generations that are identified by sociologists are:

- The Greatest Generation (1901–1927)
- The Silent Generation (1928–1945)
- Baby Boomers (1946–1964)
- Generation X (1965–1980)
- Millennials or Gen Y (1981–1995)
- Generation Z (1996–2010)
- Generation Alpha (2011–2025)

Coaches generally agree that athletes' perceptions of authority have changed in past decades. Years ago, the coach was viewed as an authoritarian figure akin to a military leader. Paul "Bear" Bryant and Bobby Knight were able to achieve a high level of success based upon strict discipline and demanding leadership.

The modern athlete seems averse to this style of coaching. Generation Z athletes desire much less direction from coaches and have access to the answers online (Wiedmer, 2015). The culture of athletics continues to change and influences the perceptions that modern athletes have toward competitive athletics, teammates, and coaches. In years past we described the dynamics of coaching as a coach-player relationship. Today we have a "triangular relationship" consisting of coach, player, and parent (Craig, 1994).

In a 2010 conference with Bobby Bowden, he responded to the question, "Coach, have kids changed?" His answer was, "Kids have not changed as much as parents have" (Bowden, 2009). In this changing environment, how does the coach retain his/her influence and relevance? Do coaches need to compromise their core beliefs to be effective in our present world?

In this modern sports climate, the concept of servant-leader coaching remains a relevant model for the contemporary coach. Evidence supports the notion that ethical core values have a significant positive effect on player motivation. Coaches still possess unique standing in our society and are widely viewed with respect. During these changing times, it is important that coaches retain this ethical sense of leading the young people of our nation. Coaches are positive influences in society when their leadership style is based on core values.

Coaching is one of the greatest opportunities to influence young people. The position of the coach is largely respected in American sports culture. Coaches possess a unique standing and sphere of influence with an audience of millions. The title "Coach" is one that is held with pride.

Maybe this is the reason why John Wooden titled his first book *They Call me Coach*. Wooden's authority was not based on pressure to conform to his policies, but rather on his referent power. His players had a reverence for him as a person. His view of leadership is revealed in his statement, "I talked to the players and tried to make them aware of what was good and what was bad. I did not try to run their lives. I think that in any group activity there has to be leadership, or it won't be successful." Coach Wooden's influence was based on the respect that he possessed rather than his position of authority. His title originated from his influence rather than from an assigned position of power.

Servant-leaders do not require a title. One of America's most eloquent authors on leadership, Ken Blanchard, said, "In the past a leader was a boss. Today's leaders must be partners with their people; they no longer can lead solely based on positional power." The servant-leader represents this shift from post-WW II authoritarian leaders to modern-day leadership that fights for the hearts of people rather than struggling for control. We serve by unlocking the potential in our relationships rather than exercising power. Our job as servant-leaders is to unlock the power that lies within the talents of our people rather than barking orders. John Maxwell said it best: "Leaders become great, not because of their power, but because of their ability to empower others." Exemplifying our values bears the weight of our influence.

My friend told me a story about a man who was unemployed. This fellow saw an ad in the newspaper, so he went to his local zoo to see if there was an opportunity. The zookeeper told him that the gorilla had died last week, and they were trying to hire a person who would dress up in a gorilla costume and impersonate an ape. The zookeeper said, "We only need you for a few weeks until the new gorilla arrives. The crowd is not very close to you, and the costume is realistic."

The pay was good, and he was so desperate that he took the job. His first day on the job he was running around, beating his chest and glaring at the visitors. The crowd was completely fooled, so he kept on the charade until the nearby lion wandered by. The impersonator was so scared at the sight of the lion that he screamed "help," to which the lion answered, "Stop screaming or you will get us both fired." (By the way, this story is a corny joke and not true!)

Unfortunately, our society contains too many leaders who pretend to be something they are not. Leadership is an important responsibility and not a charade.

Our culture needs authentic servant-leaders.

Referent Power

During the Revolutionary War, George Washington was leading his army down a road when suddenly the column stalled. Washington, sitting atop his horse, rode to the head of the column where he witnessed a young lieutenant sitting on his horse barking orders to the men on the ground. A large tree had fallen across the road, and the lieutenant was trying futilely to motivate the soldiers to move the tree.

Washington dismounted, took off his tricorn hat, removed his belt, scabbard and sword. He folded his coat across the saddle of his horse, and without these uniform symbols appeared like an ordinary soldier. He walked to the men standing shoulder-to-shoulder and said, "On my words, make your effort to move this tree." Each time he said the word "heave," the men gave their best effort. And each time, the great tree moved.

In only a few minutes, the General and his men had moved the tree from the road, and the column was able to advance. The soldiers offered a gleeful hoorah when the column began moving again. Washington carefully dressed in his coat, belted the sword across his waist, placed his hat upon his head and mounted his horse. He rode to the young lieutenant and uttered these words, "Young man, the next time you encounter an obstacle in your path, I suggest that you get down off your horse."

No servant-leader could ever receive better advice. Leadership is not about title, authority, symbols of authority or coercion—it hinges on the referent power of the leader. Our ability to inspire and influence others based upon admiration and respect is the most potent form of motivation that a coach can possess.

In the 1800's Webster defined *coach* as "a vehicle designed to transport a person of importance from where he is to where he wants to go." I submit that a successful modern coach possesses the same definition. Good coaches are transformational people in the lives of young people. The great evangelist Billy Graham once said, "A coach will impact more young people in a year than the average person does in a lifetime."

Coaches remain vehicles to transport young people, our most important resource, from where they are to where they want to go. Though written two hundred years ago, the definition of *coach* holds true today in our modern culture.

Becoming a great leader is simply the following: If we want to be leaders, we should be followers first; followers of the example of Christ—the originator of servant-leadership. Jack Welch, chairman of General Electric states, "When you become a leader, you are not given a crown. You are given a responsibility to develop other people." If you feel in your heart that coaches make a difference in lives, I submit to you that God could be calling you to follow this appeal.

Relationships

"Life is about people, not rings. Rings collect dust."

– Mark Richt

The best relationships are built upon the foundation of mutual trust. Establishing abiding relationships is the heart of coaching. Jesus' ministry was purposefully relational. The coach-player relationship is the perfect place to build strong relationships based on trust. The mutual respect that emanates from teammates is the cement that holds the culture of teamwork together.

Jesus recruited the members of his team by visiting them in their environment and presenting the invitation, "Follow Me." He visited Peter and Andrew while they were fishing; James and

John while they were in a boat with their father and Matthew while he was in a tax office. He called each member of his team individually, and they followed His call.

Coach "Bear" Bryant was one of the finest college recruiters of all time. His encounter with Lee Roy Jordan is an example of how relationships are the heart of coaching. Jordan was a great high school player, but undersized for his linebacker position. As a result, many colleges passed on him because of his size. When Bryant talked with Jordan, he told him that he might not get to play as much as he wanted because of the depth of talent that Alabama possessed. Jordan's response was, "That is ok, Coach. I want to play for Alabama because I want to be a member of a winning team."

This response struck a chord in Coach Bryant's heart. Jordan's priority was about the team and not about himself…so he played for Alabama. During his years at Alabama, the team was SEC and National Champions. The chord between these two men is an example of the tie that connects the player-coach relationship. Bryant said, "Jordan is one of the finest football players the world has ever seen." He was right about Lee Roy Jordan and coined the words, "It is not about the size of the dog in the fight, but the fight in the dog."

Servant-leader coaches must recognize the importance of relationships which help us measure the deeper attributes of our players. Through this lens, we see things that others cannot see. Servant-leadership coaching is built on relationships.

In summary, coaches who follow the principles of servant-leadership are the most relevant models of coaching in our contemporary society. Servant-leaders emphasize people above product. Servant-leadership differs from traditional forms of leadership because of the value placed upon the people within the organization. Kathleen Patterson describes servant-leadership as "follower focus" (Patterson, 2008). Robert K. Greenleaf (the father of modern servant-leadership) stresses the "care taken by the servant first to make sure that other people's highest priority needs are being served" (Greenleaf, 2008). Kristen Galek refers to servant-leadership as "leading from the heart" (Galek, 2008).

Coaching is about relationships.

The Power of Example

I firmly believe that the greatest thing you can give to another person is an example. Being a role model in our society is the most powerful form of teaching. As a coach, it is extremely important for us to exemplify what we say we believe. Actions are more influential than words. Sometimes what we do speaks so loud that people cannot hear what we say. The best teacher is a good example.

My son, Tyler, served as a "water boy" for the basketball team I coached. On the Friday morning of one of our games, I was the speaker at the 7:30am FCA huddle. My topic was, "No matter where we go, Jesus goes with us." Christ is always there with us, not only at church, but He is there in the classroom, in our games—everywhere we go.

Tyler was listening to these words, and they resonated in his heart. That evening we travelled to play one of our region foes in a pivotal game. The contest was hard fought, and the lead changed numerous times during the game. In the fourth quarter, the official called the fifth foul on my leading scorer. I argued with him, and during the heated exchange, the referee ejected me. I had to leave the gym to a chorus of boos from the spectators, and my actions certainly did not match the message that was delivered in our morning FCA Huddle.

In my absence, we lost by one point. It was a disappointing evening, and I apologized to the team in our locker room. I felt bad about the loss, but even worse that my actions contradicted everything that I preached to the team. On the drive home with my six-year-old son, Tyler, the lesson I tried to impart to my team took a much deeper, personal meaning as he said to me something I have never forgotten. "Dad, I am sorry that you and Jesus got tossed tonight."

Tyler was right, and that was the last time that "me and Jesus got tossed."

The Trust Relationship (Three Basic Questions)

The research conducted by the author to support the statements in this book on the motivational effects of servant-leadership coaching has been conducted for a decade with a sample of approximately 3,000 student-athletes. Most of these students in the sample are Generation Z (Zoomers). This research revealed that the concept of servant-leadership coaching has a positive effect on the motivational levels of high school student-athletes. Young players value trust significantly above all other coaching traits.

While young people seek adults whom they can trust, they are wary of unguarded trust. In today's world, we are conditioned to approach others with a healthy amount of skepticism because of the rampant mistrust in our lives. We must teach our players about how to build deep and abiding relationships. In our lives we encounter numerous people, so how do we know whom we can trust and how to build these relationships?

My advice on this topic has been gleaned from advice given by coaches, my parents, and pastors. In gauging the trust that underpins valuable relationships, we need to ask ourselves three questions. If the answer to any of these questions is no, it is a red flag that hinders a strong friendship.

1. Can I trust him/her?

This is the central question. If she cannot keep secrets, does not follow through with promises, proves unreliable or makes false statements, we cannot have an authentic friendship. Being aware of trust is part of self-awareness that is possibly the most important trait of a servant-leader. Sometimes our heart clouds our perspective. If we cannot trust her, we can never have an abiding relationship. Trust is more than words—it is also actions.

2. Does he/she care about me?

If they are in tune with your moods or struggles, that is a sign that they care. If they remember your birthday, your favorite food, etc., it indicates their concern for your welfare. One strong indicator is if they defend you when you are not around or to others. Emotional support from friends during times of hardship is a strong demonstration of support. Friends who forgive your mistakes are valuable assets in your life.

3. Does he/she make me better?

Surround yourself with people who see your potential and who are strong in areas where you are weak. The people who make you feel better and encourage you are hard to find. Toxic relations are constantly fraught with imbalances, as opposed to a friend who uplifts. Good friends have similar ethical values and compatible mindsets.

One great piece of advice that is appropriate in choosing friendships and facing peer pressure is to ask yourself this simple question: "Does this make me better?" If the answer is no, then why do it?! Peer pressure is sometimes a subtle factor in our lives that influences our actions. Young people can fall victim to peer pressure by choosing the wrong friends. Peer pressure is unrelenting and affects our actions.

Saying "no" is difficult for young people to do. The coach should teach how to set boundaries in behaviors. There are certain places and activities that we must counsel our players to avoid. In the world of social media, it is very easy to be entrapped. Coaches should train players to understand the implications of making online declarations and posting pictures. Everything we place online becomes permanent. College recruiters routinely check the social media footprint of players. In the modern world of social media, be careful and make friendships that are face-to-face. Online relationships can be dangerous.

Coaches are wise to teach players about friendships. For a relationship to flourish, it must take place outside of social media. Our duty is to guard our reputation and to teach our players the importance of reputation. Online peer pressure can be as dangerous as real-life peer pressure.

When we gain the trust of our players, we become much more influential. When I meet in small groups gathering information about how young players view trust, I discover that they vet us as coaches. Based on these interviews, my research indicates the presence of an antecedent to trust—trustworthiness. Trustworthiness precedes trust and involves four factors:

Antecedents to Trust (Trustworthiness)

1. Competence

> *"Leadership is a matter of having people look at you and gain confidence. If you are in control, they are in control."*
> – Tom Landry

The most basic qualifier for trust is simply professional competence. Players often refer to this as expertise. When players gather around coaches on the sideline at critical moments in the game, they are seeking guidance from their coach. When the desire to win the game is critical, trust is the essential element that wins player confidence. When the game is "on the line," our kids look to coaches whom they believe have the answer.

While coaching competence is not the only antecedent to trust, it is necessary to win the trust of the team. Without competence, complete trust cannot be gained in the minds of the team. The crucible of athletic competition is a unique atmosphere that allows the coach to win the trust that is critical in the coach-player relationship. No amount of good will can replace the fact that coaching requires a level of expertise in the sport. One of the primary duties of coaching is the constant study of the sport. We all learn how to coach from other coaches. Networking with experienced coaches is a good first step. Almost all coaches admit that everything we have learned was learned from another coach. In this profession, there is no plagiarism.

Even though a coach is a person of character and works diligently, the players expect and need a coach who has a deep knowledge of the sport. The nice coach who does not possess the expertise to lead the team will not be able to motivate players to give their maximum sustained effort. Lifetime learning is required in this field and is both an art and a science.

In addition to competence, successful coaches are more successful when they seek excellence in their players. One of the refrains in my research player interviews is their stated desire for coaches to strive for excellence. Young people want to surround themselves with adults who can make them better. In the modern-day world of athletics, players are willing to change schools to seek a program where their talents are maximized because of this strong desire to be the best they can be. The NCAA transfer portal is evidence of this phenomenon.

High school coaches are now coping with the transferability of players from one school to another. The issue of transferability will continue as a movement in athletics at every level...from youth sports to professional, and everything in between. Coaches who demonstrate an expertise to develop players will have the upper hand in recruiting and retaining athletes for their program. Young people gravitate toward coaches they believe can make them better and help them be successful.

An essential quality for an effective coach is knowledge of the game he/she is coaching. Coaches, by necessity, must understand the mechanics of coaching. Networking with other coaches is one method of acquiring a level of coaching acumen. In coaching circles, we hear a recurring phrase, "Everything I know, I learned from someone else." Borrowing ideas is a wise idea, as it is the ultimate in networking and the highest form of flattery for another coach.

2. Integrity

Young people look to their coach as a role model of character. The quickest way to lose the team's confidence is to skirt the rules or appear dishonest. Thomas Jefferson once said that "honesty is the first chapter in the book of wisdom." Servant-leadership is built on the foundation of ethical behavior. During these group interviews, they refer to integrity as "keeping your word." They mention honesty, fairness and principles in describing the integrity that precedes trustworthiness. Coaches must earn this respect from players before they can gain the team's trust. Dishonesty exhibited by the coach can destroy the foundation of trust that is essential for a strong team culture.

I was privileged to coach an amazing group of young golfers. This group of players was very talented and easy to coach. Looking back on my coaching career, it was one of the greatest periods of coaching for me. We were able to win two consecutive state championships, and after I moved to another school, this group won three more (five consecutive). They were a dynasty in our state and still discussed when golf coaches gather.

But before we won any titles and remained largely unknown, we played in a tournament in our hometown competing against three perennial golf powerhouses. The competition was extremely tough, and we were gauging our ability compared to the best teams in the state. We were confident that we could win this tournament and get on the map in our state rankings. Sure enough, we were able to win by two strokes.

It was an awesome day. The local television stations were there to cover the big win. The newspaper sports writers were interviewing players, and our guys were enjoying the limelight. It was our first big win. I normally require a stroke-by-stroke summation from each player, but on this day, since it was already dark and we were so overjoyed with our first big win, I changed our routine. I told the guys to go home, write up your stats, and we will meet tomorrow morning in the golf office before school to go over our numbers.

I took the trophy home and was basking in the glow of the big win staring at the trophy when the phone rang. The caller was one of my players who had a great day on the links and was central to our victory. His name is Carter Mize. He said, "Coach, I need to tell you something." I could tell by his voice that something was bothering him. "As I was going over my round and recording my strokes, I realized that on the fifth hole I made an error. I recorded a four, but it should have been a five." My response was, "Carter, all I ask is—are you certain?" He replied, "Coach, I have been over it in my mind several times. I made a five." My reply was, "I believe you and am very proud of your honesty for telling me this. We will go over this tomorrow morning in our meeting."

After hanging up, I double checked the rules to make sure of how we should proceed. In our matches, we always take the four lowest scores. Our score in this match was 300. The second-place team, our biggest hometown rival, scored 302. By eliminating Carter's score, and taking our next best score, we ended up with a 303—making us second place by a single stroke.

The next morning, in our team meeting I explained what happened. I began to quote a phrase that we consistently used on the team which was – "Character is doing the right thing when no one is watching." I began to address the team by saying "Character is….," and the team recited the rest of the phrase in unison. I was amazed and proud beyond words. One of the members of the team remarked, "This is no big deal. We just need to do the right thing. The trophy is not ours."

I drove over to our rival school with the trophy and gave it to the rightful winner. The coach of this team is a great friend and man of character. He said, "Coach, there are not many teams who would do this. Most would just keep it a secret and forget it…but you guys are not made that way."

In the golf office were shelves around the walls containing the trophies and plaques that the team had won. Under each trophy was a short description of the tournament, course, date, etc. But on the wall in that office, there is a conspicuous empty spot with these words: "Character is doing the right thing when no one is watching." The empty spot reminds us of what really matters in our lives—doing the right thing. This group of players was nothing short of a dynasty in high school golf. When we discuss this team and the impact they made on golf in our state, we often say, "One of the biggest trophies we ever won was the one we gave back."

Character is doing the right thing when no one is watching. Servant-leader coaches: Make this your mantra as you seek a higher standard than winning.

> *"The Lord detests lying lips, but He delights in people who are trustworthy."* – Proverbs 12:22

3. Love

"Either love your players, or get out of coaching."

– Bobby Dodd

Affection has a tremendously positive effect on player motivation. My studies have revealed a significant connection to higher levels of motivation when players feel loved by their coach. Kathleen Patterson believes that the love provided in this relationship is agape love, as described in the New Testament.

The Greek *agape* is not a feeling; it is a motivation for action that we are free to accept or reject, but God's love for us is unconditional love. In scripture the transcendent agape love is pure, willful, sacrificial love that intentionally desires another's highest good. Players give a stronger sustained effort when they view their coach as a paternal or maternal figure in their lives. Players respond positively to the affection of their coach. My firm belief is that young people desire the affection of the adults in their life.

Many articles, but few studies, exist to support the magnitude of the quality of affection in the coach-player relationship. However, one study in 2016 by *Sports and Fitness* examined the relationship between Steve Alford and Bobby Knight. Alford viewed Knight as a parent and admitted that he "sought approval from" his coach. Knight stated that coaches who seek to be father figures should be role models, since players often imitate their behaviors (UWIRE, 2016).

Atlanta Journal-Constitution writer Bernard Scott explains how Marietta High School football coach James Richards served as a life-long influence for his players. Scott titled his article "SHOULD HIGH SCHOOL COACHES HAVE TO SERVE AS FATHER FIGURES? Lifelong influence: Many enjoy becoming a role model for players." The article explored the problem of fatherless homes in our society and how the coach often substitutes as the role model for young men in our society.

Many of the social ills in our society are linked to fatherless homes. Children without fathers are four times more likely to be poor (47.6% poverty rate). Drug and alcohol abuse are "at a dramatically greater risk," according to figures from the U.S. Department of Health and Human Services. Children of single-parent homes are more than twice as likely to commit suicide (Fathers.com, 2022). "Involved fatherhood is linked to better outcomes on nearly every measure of child well-being, from cognitive development and educational achievement to self-esteem and pro-social behavior (Child and Family Research, 2022).

Coach Jimmy Sealy was the personification of a coach who loved his players. He was a traditionalist—often referred to as "old school." He was stern, but fair. Many times he helped the players on his team anonymously when they were struggling. He desired no credit but was always there when a young player was struggling. The group of players we coached on this football team were three-time state champions, and the coaching staff of five was like a family. We have remained friends for decades. When Coach Sealy retired, the word got out to the players before the state championship game. After the pregame speech, every player lined up in single file to hug the coaches as we exited the dressing room.

Each player told us they loved us as we hugged. It was a very moving scene and left us all in tears. When we warmed up before the game, I could tell that we were completely focused. We won the game that night to honor Coach Sealy. That was the night that I learned that players who love their coach will give their best effort. The love that exists on a team is a powerful motivating force, and it originates in the reverence and respect that resides in the coach-player relationship.

When Coach Sealy passed away, most of that team was present at the funeral. Coach Bill Murdock, one member of Coach Sealy's coaching tree, gave the eulogy. We stood in reverent silence as Coach Murdock described how he changed so many lives. His tough exterior often masked the tremendous heart that drove him. He truly and authentically loved all of us. He told us that constantly. He is buried in the shadow of a goalpost and has genuinely left an indelible mark on the trajectory of the lives of hundreds of young men and women in South Georgia. He was a servant-leader figure teaching many of us the principles of leading from the heart.

The characteristic that distinguished Coach Sealy above all others was that he had an uncanny ability to understand his players. He was self-aware and built a tremendous rapport with the team because of his genuine love and concern for each member of the team.

Author Jeffrey Marx wrote a book about the work of football Star Joe Ehrmann entitled *Season of Life*. Ehrmann founded the organization Coach for America (CFA) and espouses "coaching from the inside-out." He believes in the transformational impact of coaches on the lives of young men and how male coaches affect their view of authentic masculinity. One of the paragraphs from this book reveals his take on teaching young men about leadership.

"On the subject of leadership, Joe said, 'It's gotta be based on some kind of moral, ethical foundation. You can't just go with the flow in life. There's a broad road and a narrow road, and you have to learn how to courageously stand up on some kind of foundation, some kind of principle, make decisions, be a leader, and go that way. It takes great courage to lead in the right direction…and especially at the age of the boys on our football team. In the midst of all of the peer pressure, the whole social setting, it takes tremendous courage to stick to the right values, because they're often gonna find themselves at odds with the rest of their peer group" (Ehrmann, 2004).

When Ehrmann was asked, "How do you teach your players to do this?" he answered, "It must be modeled. You must give them responsibility and hold them accountable for what they do. Then you affirm what they do. That is how you teach them leadership."

Father separation syndrome is rampant in our country and has left a paternal void in our society. Homes without fathers create a negative association and create struggles with learning behaviors of children. Fathers increase the sense of well-being and stability in the family unit. Psychologists generally agree that as a result, children are more secure during the critical middle school and high school years.

One insightful quote from Andy Cook, British think-tank leader reads, "Parenting is too much of a throwaway culture, adding that we need a societal shift in perspective from regarding fathers as a dispensable extra to recognizing their value as a crucial pillar in a child's life" (Cook, 2017).

George W. Bush addressed this issue: "Over the past four decades, fatherlessness has emerged as one of our greatest social problems. We know that children who grow up with absent fathers can suffer lasting damage. They are more likely to end up in poverty or drop out of school, become addicted to drugs, have a child out of wedlock, or end up in prison. Fatherlessness is not the only cause of these things, but our nation must recognize it is an important factor" (Bush, 2018).

In the field of education, *in loco parentis* is a legal term meaning "in place of the parent." This description is appropriate in the player-coach-parent relationship and is widely accepted in the profession. This transparent effect is part of the family atmosphere that creates a culture of success on teams. Paternalistic leadership is being studied with promising outcomes in our country. Paternalistic leadership is typically defined as a leadership style that is based on fatherly benevolence combined with strong discipline and authority. When young men view their coach as a father figure, the atmosphere of the team feels more like a family, and the players are reluctant to do anything to disappoint their coach.

One of the most critical needs in our society is for young people to feel the love of an adult in their lives. Half of the members of your team will likely come from a single-parent home. Servant-leader coaches have a chance to serve as a maternal or paternal figure in the lives of those players, lending a sense of stability so important in their life.

NFL Coach Tony Dungy said, "We have a number of difficulties facing our nation, but I believe fatherlessness is right at the top of the list." We can provide a sense of value to the young people on our teams by being a parental figure in their lives. Demonstrating a loving presence in their lives is a valuable gift to young people who are missing this in their family.

Coaches—your players need your love.

4. Fairness

"I don't treat my players equally, but I treat them all fairly."

– Pat Summit

The quickest way to lose the pulse of the team is to award a player something that is not deserved. Athletics is the practice of meritocracy. Playing time is awarded on the basis of merit and must be earned—not given. In my interviews with students on subject of fairness, the feedback consists principally of four responses:

- Players trust the coach to play the best players.
- The coach must avoid favoritism.
- The policies to earn a position on the team must be established and followed precisely.
- The coach cannot succumb to pressure from parents, contributors, or outside influences

Matthew 20 presents an interesting story about the principle of fairness. In this chapter, a mother of two of the disciples came to Jesus and asked if her sons could have an elevated seat in heaven. Jesus' reply to her was that *"You do not know what you ask."*

In Mark 10, the same question is posed by James and John. Jesus' profound answer was that this *"is not for me to grant."* Christ knew that those positions must be earned—not given. When the other members of the team heard about James and John asking for favoritism, the potential for conflict was brewing. To prevent a controversy, Jesus called the team together and offered these incredible words: *"Whoever wants to be great among must be your servant, and whoever wants to be first must be last."*

These timeless words spoken by Christ to his team regarding the principle of fairness was the birth of servant-leadership. Position is not given--it must be earned.

On a lesser scale than this mother asking Jesus, sometimes coaches are pressured to grant a favorable position for one of their players. A mother's pleadings or teammates asking should not influence the decision. Coaches must realize that a position on the team must be gained with consistent effort. If players are rewarded who do not put in the work to earn their position, the overall effort of the team will diminish. Servant-leadership has tremendous motivational value if these principles guide the team. If Jesus could not grant a spot on His team, how can we as coaches think that we can?!

Even though these tenets are validated in the research, it precedes logically that people follow trustworthy leaders who care about their welfare. Remember the four antecedents to trust are: (1) expertise, (2) integrity, (3) love and (4) fairness. Young people gravitate to coaches who demonstrate authentic love and who can develop their abilities. Without the element of trust, the concept of motivation falls upon the intrinsic motivations of the players individually. The trust that exists within the context of the coach-player relationship is drawn from the concept of paternal/maternal affection. Players view the servant-leader coach much like a parent.

Coach: Treat your players like you would your own children.

CHAPTER FOUR

THE MOTIVATIONAL EFFECTS OF SERVANT-LEADERSHIP COACHING

Evidence of the motivational effects of servant-leadership has been researched by this author. During the last decade, approximately 3,000 athletes aged 13-18 were studied with the purpose of discovering what characteristics of the coach produced the motivation for these student-athletes to give their maximum sustained effort. The blueprints offered by Kathleen Patterson, research professor at Regent University, were the constructs that were surveyed in this study (Patterson, 2003).

Servant-leadership is built upon certain pillars of virtue that are central to the leader's behaviors. Patterson identifies seven virtuous constructs that she lists as: (1) altruism (2) empowerment (3) humility (4) paternal/maternal love (5) service (6) trust and (7) vision (Patterson, 2003).

- Altruism
- Empowering others
- Humility
- Love
- Service
- Trust
- Vision

Kathleen B. Patterson authored a paper entitled *Servant-Leadership: A Theoretical Model* to define the theoretical basis of servant-leadership (Patterson, 2003). Debate exists regarding the idea that servant-leadership is merely a subset of transformational leadership and not a separate, viable theory.

Kuhn suggests that the concept of transformational leadership is different from servant-leadership by arguing (Kuhn, 1970) that servant-leadership is merely an appendage of the larger concept of transformational leadership. However, Patterson eloquently defends the distinctive premise of servant-leadership which postulates that motivation to lead begins with serving.

The focus of the servant-leader is on others, while transformational leadership revolves around the leader. Patterson demonstrates that the paradox of "serving first" engenders a unique notion of leading that justifies the moniker of servant-leadership. "Somewhat paradoxical to the typical view of leadership, where the purpose is leading, servant-leaders seek to serve first as the primary means of leading" (Patterson, 2003).

Research Study

My research studied the seven constructs listed below in a series of surveys and interviews with approximately 3,000 student-athletes ages 13 to 18. This research has been conducted over a period of six years, and the sample is predominantly millennials.

Along with these young people, I also surveyed their coaches who were Generation X and Baby Boomers. My research studied the transferability of servant-leadership to the field of athletic coaching. The research discovered an existing relationship between increased player motivation and the application of a servant-leadership style of coaching.

The survey is designed to research the perceptions of high school athletes regarding their thoughts on the influence of leadership traits possessed by their coaches. The analysis offers practical insight for coaches who espouse servant-leadership.

The results demonstrate how coaches can wield this influence on their team members by the application of virtues that are imbedded in their leadership philosophy. The study has been conducted during sessions with players who were members of baseball, softball and basketball teams. The purpose of the research is to provide functional information for coaches, youth leaders, and colleagues regarding the potentially positive results of servant-leadership coaching style.

I undertook this study to gauge the effectiveness of servant-leadership coaching on the motivational level of high school athletes. The test group was comprised of 3,002 high school basketball, softball and baseball players who were participating in summer camp. The sample contained an equal number of girls and boys. The assessment instrument was a simple survey administered to each of the athletes during summer camp.

The survey was designed to determine what coaching traits served to motivate the athletes best. The study was an effort to determine a causal link between servant-leadership behaviors and increased player motivation. The seven traits which the study surveyed are (listed alphabetically):

- Altruism - Giving to others with no motive to gain something in return; kindness.
- Empowering Others - Developing/mentoring others; teaching you how to play the game of basketball.
- Humility - Focusing on other people rather than oneself; meekness.

- Love - Placing unconditional value upon the individual as a person and not what he/she offers to enable the coach to win more games; maternal/paternal affection.
- Service - Willing to assist others; helpfulness.
- Trust - Demonstrating confidence in others to succeed; keeping promises.
- Vision for the Followers - Helping team members to imagine their potential to succeed; helping others to establish goals.

Results of the survey indicate the coaching trait that provides the greatest motivational value is trust (35%). Love (16%), empowering (15%), and vision (13%) form the second tier of motivational power. Service (7%), altruism (6%) and humility (6%) possess the least motivational value. (Durden, 2016)

Seven Constructs of Servant-Leadership Coaching

(1) Altruism

Altruism is recognized as a kindly benevolence, denoting a sense of selflessness and contains an element of sacrificial service that originates in the need to treat others as we wish to be treated. Altruism is synonymous with the biblical admonition, *"So whatever you wish that others would do to you, do also to them...."* (Matthew 7:12).

Recognizing the need of others and then helping them is the embodiment of altruism. Servant-leaders who seek to serve first are evidence of this construct. "Servant-leaders look for an attitude of humility and modesty along with selflessness and altruism--an approach which seeks what is best for others rather than the leader himself" (Patterson, 2003).

The person who introduced me to the concept of servant-leadership was Bill Turner. His life as a philanthropist has made a tremendous impact on Columbus, Georgia, where I reside. His belief in the transformational power of servant-leadership was evident in everything he did. My introduction to the theory of servant-leadership was the result of receiving a book written by him, entitled *The Learning of Love: A Journey Toward Servant-Leadership*.

Bill Turner was the past chairman of Synovus Financial Corporation, founder of the Pastoral Institute, member of the Georgia Board of Regents, trustee at Emory University, Treasurer of the W. C. Bradley Company, and resident of Columbus, Georgia. Mr. Turner, with his many accolades, often described himself as a Sunday school teacher for more than 50 years.

In his book, Mr. Turner described his life journey through the lens of a servant-leader. The researcher's views on servant-leadership are profoundly influenced by the philosophy of Bill Turner, as this introduction to servant-leadership was the wellspring of my personal philosophy. Mr. Turner's mentorship was transformational in my life and has led to the research that is validated in the concepts of servant-leadership coaching. He is the best example I know of a person who practiced altruism in his life.

The call to coach involves giving. The coaches I know are constantly giving to their players with rides, equipment, food... It is a universal characteristic of the profession. If Coach Clyatt had not given me those cleats, it is very likely this book would not have been written. When a player has a need, the coaches step up to help. One of the most difficult aspects of coaching is the amount of time that is given to young people, often to the neglect of quality time with our own families. Coaching requires a spouse who also believes in the importance of this career.

(2) Empowerment

Empowerment is synonymous to developing people. The servant-leader coach believes empowerment is the crux of coaching. The coach who empowers others in this process actually transfers a portion of power that is often reserved for the top rung of traditional leadership.

Robert K. Greenleaf is referred to as "the father of the empowerment movement" (Russell, Stone, 2002). In one of his last writings, Greenleaf asked the questions, "Do those served grow as persons? Do they, while being served, become healthier, wiser, freer, more autonomous, more likely themselves to become servants?" (Greenleaf, 1977).

His theory purported that the central element of leading flows from a mutual sense of trust. Bill Manning described a "resonant trust between the leader and the follower, which can only be achieved reciprocally through individual empowerment...." (Manning, 2004).

The development progression that occurs between player and coach is essentially the mentoring process. The very essence of coaching is an exchange of knowledge between the coach and the player. Russell describes the process as enabling others by "not hoarding the power they have but by giving it away" (Russell, 2001). Empowerment is the heart of this knowledge exchange as the coach enables the player to act independently.

One desired outcome of servant-leader coaching is that players will become coaches themselves. The empowering process is analogous to an apprenticeship. In this relationship, the teacher allows an increasing freedom to the apprentice as he/she learns the profession. As the apprenticeship continues, the pupil is given the freedom to make more decisions until he/she becomes capable of acting autonomously.

Good leaders are not measured by how many followers they have, but rather how many leaders they produce. The coach who translates the ability to think independently in his/her absence understands their duty to empower others. If we as coaches do a good job of empowering our team, they will not need us.

(3) Humility

"Humility is not thinking less of yourself; it is thinking of yourself less." —C. S. Lewis

Humility is focusing on others rather than oneself. It is antithetical to a dictatorial style of leadership. Servant-leadership is free of arrogance or bombastic attributes. Patterson notes that humility "counteracts" self-interest (Patterson, 2003). The servant-leader coach practices an authentic interest in others and demonstrates a focus on the accomplishments of the team over himself.

Bear Bryant emulated this sense of humility as he gave praise to others after wins but took the blame himself for losses. "When we win it is us, but when we lose it is me" was the message Coach Bryant preached (Reed, 1994). The quality of meekness is sometimes confused with weakness, but when practiced authentically is a sense of strength under control.

Humility is a rare form of courage possessed by servant-leader coaches who seek to stand at the end of the line rather than in the forefront. John Wooden referred to the trait of "selflessness" in his *Pyramid of Success*. Wooden believed in an eagerness (as opposed to a willingness) to "sacrifice personal glory or gain...." (Wooden, 2005).

If you only remember one thing from this book, the following point is perhaps it. The star of every successful team is the team. Individuals don't win games; teams do" (Wooden, 2005).

> *"In the same way, you who are younger, submit yourselves to your elders. All of you, clothe yourselves with humility toward one another, because, God opposes the proud but shows favor to the humble."*
>
> — I Peter 5:5

Perhaps one of the greatest examples of humility can be seen on the day the great running back Emmitt Smith was inducted into the Pro Football Hall of Fame. On the day that was his, he deferred much of the credit for his achievements to others. He began his speech by paying tribute to Walter Payton, whose yardage record he surpassed. He thanked all of his coaches, notably his high school coaches. Perhaps one of the greatest tributes he handed to a teammate was the thank you he gave to Daryl Johnston, the fullback who blocked for him during his career with the Dallas Cowboys. His remark to Johnston was, "Without you, there is no me."

Smith took very little credit for his records, but rather gave the credit to others. This moving speech is a classic example of how authentic humility is the foundation of true strength. As Spencer Kimball said, "Humility is royalty without a crown." No person ever stands so tall as when he leans to help another. It is not a sign of weakness, but rather a show of legitimate power. Great leaders give credit to others.

One interesting note regarding humility is that research indicates that young people do not value humility as much as other virtues surveyed in our studies. This link seems to be unique to millennials, as Generation X rates humility higher. In her book *Radical Humility,* Sarah Buss writes, "The increase in self-esteem has corresponded to a decrease in humility… The greater tendency to think well of oneself has corresponded to the tendency to think more of - and about - oneself than one thinks of - and about - anyone else" (Buss, 2020).

We all have a gravitational pull to our own self-interest, and a corresponding difficulty in being aware of the welfare of others. Troy Jollimore, professor of philosophy, expressed this opinion: "People have a hard time listening to each other. They find it hard to treat people with whom they disagree with respect or to take diverging views seriously. They have so much self-confidence in their own opinions that they are unable to be self-critical, and the existence of people who hold different opinions strikes them as disturbing, as a kind of affront."

The antidote to this emphasis on ourselves is to practice self-awareness. Many leaders believe that he most important trait of a servant-leader is self-awareness. Humility seems to be waning in our modern society, but coaches who practice authentic humility are positioned to influence young people about the value of true humility.

It is not about me.

(4) Love

Agapao love as defined by Patterson is "the cornerstone of servant-leadership" (Patterson, 2003). It is rooted in the Greek language and describes the deep affection connecting two people. Winston defines agapao love as "doing the right thing at the right time for the right reason" (Winston, 2015). Servant-leadership is a leadership style based upon a moral code guiding servant-leaders to do what is morally right and virtuous. Servant-leadership coaches seek a higher standard of moral influence.

Winston teaches that love is a noun, but agapao love is a verb (Winston, 2015). Love is a concept, while agapao love is the practice of this concept. Agapao is action-oriented, and love is conceptual. If we as coaches love our players, our actions will demonstrate that to them. Winston conjectures that agapao embodies a paternalistic or maternal obligation, theorizing that players who view their coach as a substitute parent retain more respect for the coach.

Winston writes that the resultant effect of agapao love practiced by the servant-leader coach produces "higher performance by the follower towards achieving the leader's goals" (Winston, 2015).

Mark Richt explained this concept in his description of Bobby Bowden as, "He loved us as coaches, and he loved the players, and we knew it. And we loved him for that," Richt said, "When it came to winning games and stuff, we wanted to win for him as much as we wanted to win for us, because we loved him so much." This paternalistic love that Bowden's players felt was the rallying point for his teams. The teams that have love at the core of their culture are highly motivated to give their best during times of adversity and competition. Love is the glue that bonds the togetherness on teams.

In Paul Harvey's tribute on the death of Vince Lombardi, he said, "The men who alternately loved Lombardi and hated him, would walk through fire for him…and today they are lined up to pay respect to the coach that made them champions." He was deeply loved by the men who played for him. Lombardi believed that if the members of a team loved each other, they played together as a team. He urged his players to "be men for others and to serve others." Coach Lombardi once stated on national television that, "We don't like each other; we love one another" (Mastro, 1996).

Relationships built on love are permanent and able to withstand the storms of life that we encounter. One of the greatest biblical passages to describe the culture of love on a team is 1 Corinthians 13:4-5. *"Love is patient, love is kind. It does not envy, it does not boast, it is not proud. It does not dishonor others, it is not self-seeking, it is not easily angered, it keeps no record of wrongs."* We should strive for this description in our Christian walk, in our marriage, in our family, in our profession and in our relationships. Love is the foundation of our faith. God loved us enough to send His son to die for our sins. Love is the centerpiece to any strong relationship and is the foundation for extraordinary teamwork in athletics.

(5) Service

Service is the natural outcome of being a servant-leader. Service is a resultant core behavior of the servant-leadership philosophy. Patterson believes service "is the primary function of a type of leadership that is not based on one's own interests…." (Patterson, 2003). Service is the act of choosing others first. It is the behavior of generosity. Winston writes, "Service is the heart of servant-leadership theory" (Farling, Stone, Winston, 1999).

The act of serving is when the leader forfeits authority or privilege for the sake of followers (Matteson, Irving, 2015). Greenleaf's seminal statement appropriately describes the act of service that is central to the theory of servant-leadership. "The servant-leader is servant first…. It begins with the natural feeling that one wants to serve first. Then conscious choice brings one to aspire to lead" (Greenleaf, 1977).

My research does not indicate that high school athletes value service to a large degree. Respondents indicate a tepid 7% ranking on the survey. Many schools adopt programs of servant-leadership but only feature the service aspect of the philosophy. Do not confuse service with servant-leadership. Servant-leadership is much more than service. The philosophy of servant-leadership is widely adopted by businesses, schools, and coaches but remains largely misunderstood. Leaders mistakenly create service projects and believe that they are servant-leadership organizations.

Servant-leadership is about creating leaders who develop the people in their organizations—not just outreach programs. Service programs are vital to our nation and are very helpful for a large segment of our nation, but they are only one segment of servant-leadership. The philosophy of servant-leadership is intended to develop the talents of people by creating opportunities to empower them, set a vision for their lives, affirm them as persons of worth and to change the community as a result. Service programs are excellent tools to assist people in need, but they do not constitute servant-leadership organizations. As servant-leaders, we should endorse programs of service while realizing that servant-leadership is much more than service alone.

When I began to research the motivational effects of servant-leadership, I realized that much misunderstanding exists about what the philosophy is. As coaches and leaders, it is incumbent upon us to educate our people about the tremendous transformational power of servant-leadership. We do this by understanding the philosophy and emulating it in our lives. Acts of service are a great demonstration of our compassion for others, and servant-leader coaches have a rare opportunity to teach players that service is incumbent upon us in our Christian walk.

We help others as a result of our gratitude.

(6) Trust

Trust is the strongest element of the servant-leadership philosophy. Trust is essential for human relationships to flourish. The ultimate goal of the servant-leader is to demonstrate genuine compassion for others by the establishment and maintenance of a trust relationship. Cho and Ringquist (2010) present trust as an outcome and not a process. Trust is the result of three input behaviors that leaders demonstrate: competence, benevolence, and integrity. Trusted leaders are perceived as possessing these three precursors, establishing *trustworthiness*. Leaders who consistently possess *trustworthiness* have the ability to gain the trust of followers (Cho, Ringquist, 2010). Organizational outcomes follow leaders who are perceived as trustworthy.

Research by Harjinder, Boies, Finegan & McNally (2005) support the theory of antecedent behaviors that help to create trust. Predispositions of the trustee, including perceived ability, benevolence, and integrity are the factors that create an "intention to trust" in the disposition of the trustor. Positive work attitudes are linked to a trust relationship between the leader and followers (Harjinder, Boies, Finegan & McNally, 2005). Mayer (1995) explains the relationship between trustor (individual trusting) and trustee (individual being trusted) as a "willingness to be vulnerable to the actions of another" (Mayer, 1995).

In our contemporary society, many of the pillars of trust have been undermined. We live in a skeptical word as a result. Many of the institutions such as churches, news media, government leaders and coaches have been tainted with scandals. Young people are afraid to offer unguarded trust to these venerable factions that were formerly easy to believe. The coach in our society still possesses a platform of influence and is viewed with respect. My admonition to my coaching colleagues is to guard this position and maintain the trust of those we serve. We have a powerful position of impact, and we need to protect our standing by ensuring that our behavior displays a higher standard of ethics. The high privilege of coaching should never be used to gain favor or manipulate the circumstances to our advantage.

Coach, earn the trust of the team.

"Therefore do not let what is for you a good thing be spoken of as evil."

—Romans 14:16

(7) Vision

Vision is the ability of the leader to see inherent worth and value in others. Vision looks forward to the ultimate destination. Servant-leaders look forward to the innate potential of individual people within the organization and seek to "assist each one in reaching that state" (Patterson, 2003). Vision for servant-leaders requires an eye upon the future potential of each person under their care.

A study performed by Berson (2001) links higher levels of confidence and optimism to leaders who cast concise vision statements (Berson, 2001). Looking forward to dream of what possibilities exist for others is an act of vesting purpose and trust in followers. The exchange between mentor and mentee in this relationship is an act of demonstrating confidence in the follower that provides a sense of direction. Perhaps Margaret Wheatley says it best by stating, "The real fuel in leadership is believing in other people. I define a real leader as someone who has great faith in people's ability and who uses every opportunity to create means for them to offer their creativity to the organization (Schieffer, 2003)."

One of the blind spots for many coaches is explained by the theory of self-fulfilling prophecy. A self-fulfilling prophecy, according to sports psychologists, is a mindful expectation from a coach about the potential of his/her player. When we as coaches assess the ability of a player without realizing it, we send subconscious signals to the player. This unconscious bias sets in motion a series of events that ultimately causes the coach's original prediction to become true.

Unintentionally, we may interact less with this athlete by providing less feedback and thus establishing lower expectations. Developing an early bias causes us to deliver less praise and informational or corrective feedback. If not careful, we can attribute the athletes' mistakes to lack of ability and their successes to luck. These moments are termed differential encounters. Many good coaches unintentionally fall prey to the notion of self-fulfilling prophecies. Incumbent upon the coach is the obligation to objectively assess each player and reserve judgment as long as possible, knowing that we must decide who receives playing time.

Servant-leader coaches constantly guard themselves against forming conclusions about a player too soon. Helping each player to establish goals is part of the process of improvement. Coaches who spend time with players to help them establish realistic goals for their lives is time well spent. Goal setting is part of the process of knowing our players.

The Path-Goal Theory is especially useful in clarifying a sense of mission and purpose for each player. This theory originated in the writings of Martin Evans (1970). He posits that the leader's job is to help team members find the best path to reach their dreams. For this to happen, the leader must let each player know their roles on the team. Servant-leader coaches provide the confidence and direction for each person to attain their aspirations. The goals should be balanced between challenging (elevating) and reachable.

Therefore, the creation of goals should be a collaborative exercise between the student-athlete and coach. The central purpose of the servant-leader coach is to help people as they define and reach their milestones. The leader helps the player define the path and install the milestones along the path to success.

These milestones are clearly defined and should be measured along the journey to reach the ultimate challenge. A clear sense of role expectations increases the likelihood of reaching the goal. Clear communications and feedback between player and coach are necessary to achieve the target. Ultimately, the Path-Goal Theory is relational in nature. Developing and empowering players is the purpose of this goal-setting task.

CHAPTER FIVE

TEN THOUSAND SHOTS

"A goal with no plan is just a wish."
– Lynwood Mock

One of the most vivid examples of a coach who transformed my life occurred when I was a freshmen in high school. I attended elementary school and junior high in my hometown of Attapulgus, GA. When our class entered high school, we were consolidated into a new and much larger county school. It was a large school, and we knew very few of the students who became our classmates. The members of my new team had been our opponents in prior years. I was moved from being the "big fish in a small pond" to the "small fish in a big pond," as one of my coaches explained.

When I played basketball for this new school, I had a very mediocre freshman year. I was disappointed and discouraged. But one morning I received a note from the varsity coach. He requested an audience with me in his office. He talked to me the entire period about basketball and setting goals to improve as both a player and a person. This conversation was decades ago, but one thing he said to me, I will never forget. Coach Mock said, "There is nothing wrong with you that 10,000 shots won't fix."

Walking back to class, my mind began to devise a plan. Little did I realize that Coach Mock was defining my path to reach a goal I dreamed about. That afternoon after school, I jogged to my old junior high gym with a basketball. I began shooting and discovered that I could shoot ten shots per minute (one shot every six seconds). This was quite a pace, but I was able to shoot 300 shots that day in less than an hour. I figured ten shots a minute, 100 shots in ten minutes, 300 shots in 30 minutes; 300 shots M-Th for 1,200 per week was the pace I needed. It was work, but almost immediately I began to see progress.

For the next few months my confidence increased, and my shooting accuracy improved dramatically. I recorded every workout in a black notebook with percentages, number of shots and even timed the workouts. These were the mileposts that are important in the Path-Goal Theory. One thing of importance was that I set a date to finish and a schedule. My goal was to hit 70% of 10,000 shots. Ultimately, I was able to actually make 10,000 shots and exceeded my goal by a few thousand. It was a period in my life that made a huge difference. So much so, that I became a basketball coach and have enjoyed my career for decades. The meeting with Coach Mock changed the trajectory of my life. A clearly defined path to reach these goals made the difference. I will never forget it.

But there is another chapter to this story. One brisk October morning, I was walking into the athletic office when I heard someone crying. I walked around the corner and there, sitting on the floor with his face in his hands sat Jim Sizemore, a seventh grade student. As I walked toward him, I saw the new basketball roster posted on the wall above his head, and his name was not on it. He did not make the team.

Jim was a great athlete, and I was surprised he did not make the roster but knew that the coach made this tough decision, and Jim needed someone to encourage him and not make excuses for him. So the first thing that came to my mind was, "Well Jim, are you going to sit here and cry, or do you want to do something about this?" He looked up and said, "Coach, I am willing to put in the work. I really wanted to be on the team."

When we walked into the office, the first thing I said to him was, "Jimbo, there is nothing wrong with you that 10,000 shots won't fix." So we devised some goals and navigated a path for for Jim, and he committed to doing them. We wrote it down together, and Jim took the list of goals with him. Just a few days later, Jim's father called to say he was building a basketball goal and court at their house. Jim began working every day. I could sense a change in his attitude and see his confidence building. We visited his house one weekend and watched him shooting, running, doing plyometrics, resistance running—all of the things that were written on his goal sheet. He was making great progress.

In June, our team attended Atlanta Superstar Basketball Camp. During that time it was the biggest and best camp in the southeast. Jim had a great week. He was clearly one of the best 8th graders at the camp. When awards were given, Jim was given the Best Player Award for the entire camp. I was amazed at this kid who came from a 7th grader who did not make the cut to the best player at the best camp in just a few short months. It was amazing how the path he devised and executed improved his skills. When basketball season began, Jim was playing incredibly. He was the best player we had on the team.

On Thanksgiving our team had an FCA Hay Ride on the Sizemore's farm. It was a great event ending with a bonfire where every student who wanted to stood before their teammates and told the group what they were thankful for. Jim stood there and said that he was thankful for his mother's prayers. He said that his mom always prayed that when he did something wrong at school he would get caught. I chuckled to myself, because her prayers were working. He finished his words with this statement: "There is something about a mother's prayers."

During the Christmas holidays, we practiced basketball. I coached the varsity boys, and Jim's JV team practiced right before us each day. When I arrived and walked into the gym, I noticed it was eerily silent. I could hear no sounds of balls bouncing or sneakers squeaking. There was a group of players on the end of the court crowded around Jim, who was lying on his back. I rushed to him and began CPR but could not detect a pulse or breathing. While trying to resuscitate him, I was praying with all my heart, "Please God, do not let this young man die!"

In just a few minutes the ambulance arrived. My wife and I followed them to the emergency room with his sister, Kena. We were anxiously waiting and praying when his mother and father arrived. His father went back into the room but came back with the news that Jim had passed. His mom dropped to her knees in the waiting room and earnestly prayed aloud for God to save her son. I remembered Jimbo's words, "There is something about a mother's prayers."

Jim was buried on a bright winter day surrounded by his teammates, friends and coaches. His death affected many of the students and teachers in our school very deeply. Many of his friends were so inspired by his death that they were baptized, rededicated their lives, and some accepted Christ. His life was an example of his faith that impacted many lives.

Jim was my son Chip's hero and a great example to emulate. He was a great role model for his teammates and was beloved by everyone who knew him. He was one of the most inspirational players I ever coached. His number 14 still reserves a special place in my heart to the extent that it is only issued to players who will wear it with distinction and provide a good example for teammates. In my heart, #14 is revered and deserves a unique spot. Number 14 made me a better coach. Not many weeks pass that I do not think about him.

After the funeral, my wife Diane and I went to the Sizemore Farm to pay our respects to his family. As we walked up their driveway, we saw the basketball goal where Jim made 10,000 shots. His mother met us and asked us to come to Jim's room where she wanted to show us something. It was a typical teenager's room with sports posters on the walls and containing all the things that a teenage athlete would find interesting.

But pinned on the wall over his bed was a list of his goals. It was the list that we wrote that morning in October when Jim discovered he did not make the team. Mrs. Sizemore told me how Jim worked every day and followed the list precisely. His parents were rightfully proud of Jim's efforts to make the team and respected how he worked every day. Mrs. Sizemore handed me the list, and I have kept it in my Bible since that time. Jim's life made a huge difference!

Jim taught me that our players need goals. I learned that goals have to be (1) reachable (2) measurable (3) scheduled and (4) written. When you are helping players to set goals, these four points are a great template. Jim Sizemore taught us much about the value of hard work and following our goals. Sometimes the teacher becomes the student in our positions as mentors. Jim Sizemore taught me much more than I taught him, and he did that without words.

The most important issue regarding goal setting is to make sure that our goals align with God's plan in our lives. Before setting goals, we should pray for wisdom and direction. The legendary Bobby Richardson, second-baseman for the New York Yankees, was one of my childhood idols. Richardson won five straight Gold Gloves, appeared in four World Series, winning the series three times, and was named World Series MVP. He played in the All-Star game seven times and has been named to the Yankees Hall of Fame. He is an ardent supporter of the Fellowship of Christian Athletes and a frequent speaker for them.

After watching the movie *The Pride of the Yankees*, Richardson set as his goal to play second base for the Yankees. That movie about the life of Lou Gehrig made an indelible impression in Richardson's life. Ironically, he was awarded the Lou Gehrig Award after he retired at the young age of 31 to spend more time with his family. He was a very successful college baseball coach in addition to his professional career, and he remains one of the most popular Yankees of all time. When asked to pronounce the benedictory prayer at an FCA banquet, his prayer reflected his belief in the power of aligning personal goals with God's will. His words were:

"Lord, your will. Nothing more, nothing less, nothing else."

—Bobby Richardson

CHAPTER SIX

RESEARCH CONCLUSIONS

Based on the research I have conducted since 2016, I believe the concept of servant-leadership coaching has a positive effect on the motivational levels of high school basketball players. Young players value trust significantly above all other coaching traits. The concept of trustworthiness involving: (1) competence (2) integrity (3) paternal/maternal love, and (4) fairness offers the most significant positive effect on player motivation.

Of the seven constructs, players value trust far above other coach behaviors. Love, empowerment, and vision possess similar but less value in the perceptions of high school athletes. From these results, I conclude that young people desire leaders who are trustworthy, who love them, who have the ability to develop them as people and athletes, and who see innate potential in them.

Even though these principles are validated in the research, it precedes logically that people follow trustworthy leaders who care about their welfare. Research further implies that high school players gravitate to coaches who demonstrate authentic love, and who can develop their abilities. Without the element of trust, the concept of motivation falls upon the intrinsic motivations of the players individually. The trust that exists within the context of the coach-player relationship is drawn from the concept of paternal/maternal affection. Players view the servant-leader coach much like a parent.

The servant-leadership philosophy is a growing movement within the coaching fraternity. After decades of coaching, I chose to study this idea since little literature exists to validate the value of servant-leadership related to athletic coaching. Coaches emulate servant-leader constructs without knowing the worth of their ideas and the positive effect this style has on player motivation. The profession of coaching offers an opportunity for meaningful change in the lives of others. I believe that coaches occupy a prominent platform with the potential to be life-changing, transformational influences for young people. Coaches who choose to make a positive difference are wise to study the effects of servant-leadership coaching.

Building trust is a gradual process and involves social interactions between two people that prove the predictability and dependability of each other. In the coach-player relationship, the antecedents that factor into the trust vetting process are as mentioned earlier: competence, love (paternal/maternal affection), fairness and integrity. The presence of these mutual elements allows both parties in the relationship to regulate the extent of commitment. Dependence upon other teammates is the hallmark of a healthy culture. When one team member can count on his/her teammates to contribute their best effort to the program, a healthy culture will follow.

A study of the coach-player trust relationship for soccer players indicates that paternalistic authority has more motivational value than authoritarian coaches. Collegiate soccer players in this study viewed the benevolence exhibited by their coach as a stronger motivational indicator (Li, 2021). Young people tend to gravitate to coaches who care about them and who depend less on authoritarian structures. This study supports the notion that

"Kids do not care how much you know until they know how much you care."

We should treat our players like they are our children.

Research Illustration (Columns)

The columns below illustrate the opinions of our sample group. The blue column represents the students who selected that construct as their first choice. In other words, blue represents the trait of the coach that motivates them the most. Red is the representation of their second choice, and green shows the third choice. As you can see by examining the columns, the first choice of trust is twice as powerful as the first choice of the next construct. In fact, the second choices of trust are stronger than the first choices of all others except empowerment. The graphic tells us just how powerful the element of trust is in the coach-player relationship.

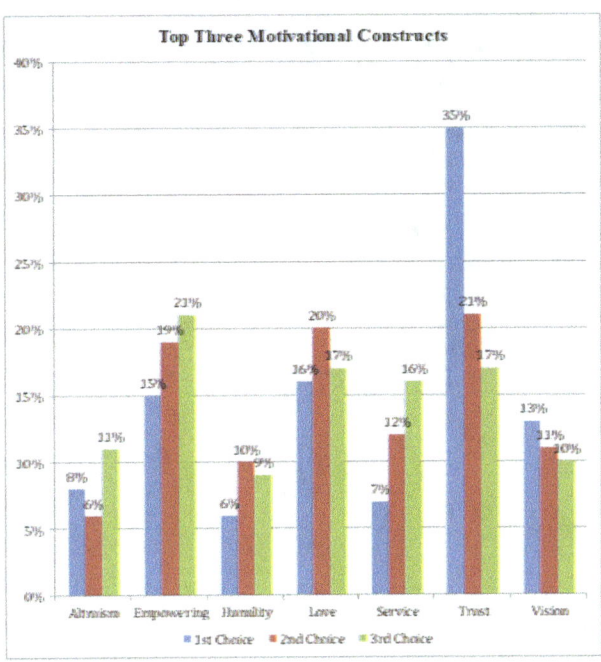

Research Illustration (Pie Chart)

The pie chart is an illustration of how trust is valued by young people. Building trust is the key to creating a team that is highly motivated. Players will give their best effort if they believe in their leader and will sustain their efforts in the face of adversity. The will to win that is so important on teams is built on the foundation of trust. Trust is the tie that binds teams together.

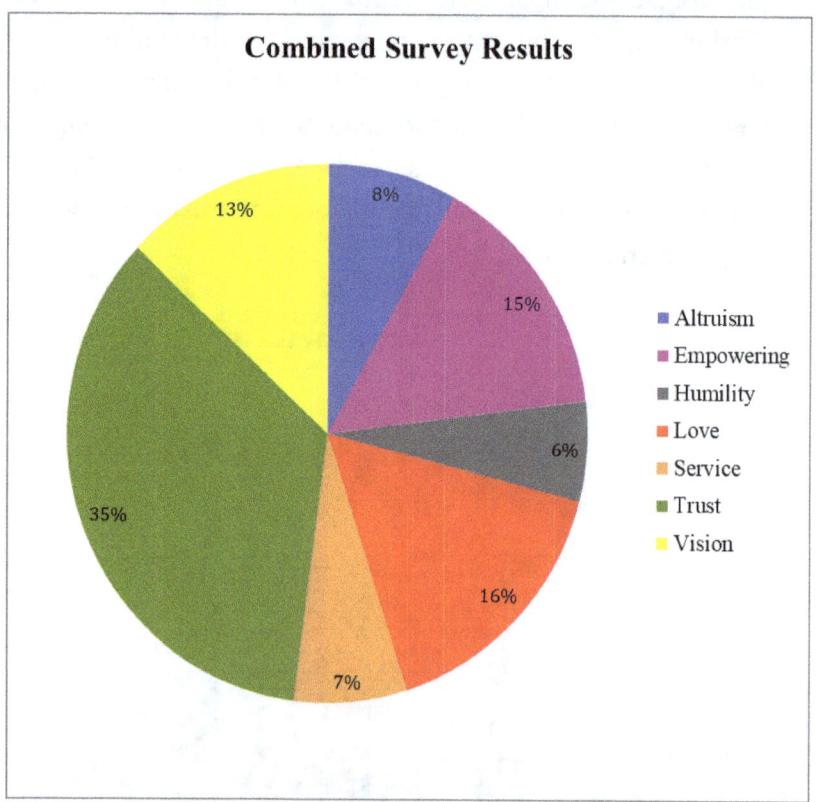

CHAPTER SEVEN

THE COACH AS A TEACHER

Empowering players comes down to teaching. The impact of the coach's teaching prowess is what players require to become independent of the coach. Remember, our duty is to help build young people who will not need us at some point in their lives. One of the most difficult tasks of coaches is to say goodbye to players we love and have worked side-by-side with for many years.

We are like ship builders who select hearty timbers, strong sails, and build ships that withstand the storms of life. We help build young people who are water tight and rugged, yet responsive to the changing winds of life. We teach them how to navigate the storms and high seas, preparing them for the journey to their chosen destination. When all is finished, we stand on the shore and wave goodbye, telling them we will keep the lighthouse burning so they will have a reference point to return to their home shore. When they come back home, we celebrate their achievements and assume the role of mentor in their lives when needed. Our job is to help young people learn the game we love and how to be a better person as a result of our relationship. Coaching is about empowering our athletes via teaching. And the heart of teaching is feedback.

One piece of advice I give to coaches is to study the teaching methods of John Wooden, who was one of the best ever. His theory regarding skill acquisition is a four-part process.

1. Explanation
2. Demonstration
3. Imitation
4. Repetition, Repetition, Repetition, Repetition

The most instructive article regarding Wooden's methods of coaching was conducted by Ronald Gallimore and Roland Tharp. This article is a must-read for coaches at all levels and reveals the simplistic yet influential methods of coaching (teaching) athletes.

Wooden explained his style to observe practice, and when he spotted an error, he would reduce the distance between himself and the player. He would speak in a mild voice, stop the practice and provide what is referred to as a "correction sandwich." This method was to (M+) model the correct way to perform the skill, (M-) demonstrate the way they were doing it, and (M+) model the correct technique again. M- is a negative correction, and M+ is a positive reinforcement.

These feedbacks lasted approximately four seconds. When interviewing Wooden's players, they believed that his feedback during these "sandwiches" was received positively because it was actionable and helped their understanding of what he expected. Wooden believed that positive instruction was the secret to learning. His words were usually, "Here is the way to do it. (M+). Here is how you are doing it (M-). Here is how I want you to do it (M+)."

Each of these statements was demonstrated or modeled visually to the player. During the 74-75 season, these two researchers coded 2,356 discrete utterances which they felt were easy to code. Wooden seldom used lectures or long talks to teach his team. These teaching moments were frequent and brief.

These brief methods he utilized were often referred to as instructions or utterances.

Of these moments, 6.9% were compliments, 6.6% were expressions of displeasure and 75% were positive feedback in the form of "the sandwich." Wooden's practices were non-stop, intense, demanding and quick, so that the games moved slower than the practices. The majority of his expressions of displeasure were embedded with instruction. He would scold and re-instruct simultaneously. Wooden believed that the coach is a teacher and provides feedback in the form of modeling, re-instructing and informing. His methods were masterful in their substance, and I beg every coach to study them.

Wooden's teaching methods have been researched by educators and sports psychologists. Positive instruction characterized his practices. He avoided emotional outbursts and assumed the role of the expert instructor. Instruction should be delivered objectively without emotion, and each correction should contain the coach's expectation. Wooden believed in visuals during these times… He demonstrated how the motion should look. Many golf instructors nationwide utilize this same method, utilizing videos as examples.

The power of image accompanied by words is a compelling feature of good teachers. A coach once told me that people remember 10% of what you tell them, 10% of what you show them, but 80% of what you show *and* tell them. Whether factually accurate of not, this statement is an effective teaching tool. Many of the most effective teachers utilize a method called *kinesthetic learning,* a style in which skill acquisition takes place by the students carrying out the motion of a selected physical activity accompanied by listening to a coach or watching demonstrations. This method provides immediate feedback (which is central to skill acquisition) from the coach and corrects the flaws in the motion of the athlete.

This is a popular method for golf instructors whereby they observe the student's swing, make corrective demonstrations, allow the student to adjust their swing and repeat. The feedback of the instructor is critical to success in this method. The dictionary defines kinesthesia as "the ability to know where the parts of your body are and how they are moving."

Kinesthetic learning links the process of learning to physical activity. It is a learning style during which the learner has to feel or move in order to learn more effectively. Also referred to as hands-on, or physical learning, kinesthetic learning combines the three other main learning styles: visual, auditory, and tactile learning (Bay Atlantic University, 2022).

CHAPTER EIGHT

OUTSIDE THE LINES

Family

The first institution that God created was family. A man and woman were the first human elements that God introduced in His creation. Coaching demands much of our time, often to the neglect of our family. Coaches need to intentionally make time with family a priority.

In my career, most of the regrets I have are because I did not spend enough time with my family and get involved in the lives of my children. When we are so focused on our profession, it is difficult to detach from the intensity of coaching and give our full attention to our families. We all know the feeling of leaving practice or a game with unanswered questions. Even though it is difficult to change these mental gears, we must be available to our families when we are home. Our need for compartmentalization in our lives is the secret to accommodating this important potential blind spot in the coach's life.

Coach's Spouse

The modern coach in contemporary society needs a strong marriage to weather the storms of the coaching profession. The ups and downs of coaching can create undue stress in marriages. When we come home from practice or games, it is very difficult to decompress and become a loving husband or wife. Carrying this burden of stress is unhealthy for coaches and harmful to marriages. The pressure of coaching can be overwhelming. Fear of failure, pressure to win, concern for our players, burnout, lack of family… are some of the issues on a long list of conditions that coaches face in our society.

The accumulative of external forces can wreak havoc on the coach's family. In my life, my spouse has been the rock that steadies me during the crucible of athletic competition. If Diane had never bought into my calling, I would never have been successful in this career. Coaching requires a deep and abiding partnership. It is a twin call; the coach and his/her spouse are together in the decision to coach.

One cold winter night long ago, my basketball team journeyed to play a game against a very good team. We had some injuries and were missing some key players for this decisive road game. The entire game was a battle with the raucous crowd responding to every play. Our players suffered through the jeers of the hostile crowd. At one point in the game, an inebriated fan confronted one of my young players on the bench. I stopped the game until he was removed. It was a wild night!

We were able to find a slim lead, and with just a few minutes remaining, Heath Varnedoe was able to make two free throws to win the game. In the face of the hostility, security told my players to dispense with the handshakes and go straight to the locker room to avoid any potential incidents. I ushered the guys off the floor and was looking around the gym to make sure all the guys were accounted for when I realized that I was surrounded by spectators from the other school. They were jostling and crowding around me, preventing me from exiting the gym floor. I could sense the hostility like electricity and was "squeezed in" when I was confronted by the intoxicated fellow that I had removed from the gym. In the words of *O Brother, Where Art Thou*, I was in a tight spot.

As I was trying to graciously remove myself, I noticed over this fellow's shoulder that the crowd behind him parted slightly. This caught my attention, and as I focused on the movement, I saw it part further as someone was forcing their way into the crowd. I was wondering, "Is someone coming to my rescue?"—when I realized it was my wife, Diane. To my amazement, she was moving in to save me totally unafraid!

It was one of those moments in life when she demonstrated her unconditional love regardless of the danger and was willing to fight through that crowd for her husband. I will never forget Diane fighting through that crowd to stand beside me during a very tense time. The spouse's support is the backbone of the coach's call.

Diane has endured the ups and downs of the coaching profession with me. We have been married for decades and enjoy a unique partnership. Without her support, nothing would have worked right in this career. We were married on April 1st (April Fool's Day). When we tell people this, we get that quizzical look where they are thinking, "Who would actually get married on that day?" We tell them that with my poor memory, it is a day no one could ever forget, and if we ever wanted to split, we could just say "April Fool" and no hard feelings…

Of course this is a joke, Dear Reader. Our marriage is about as solid as one can be because we made a commitment on that day years ago. Marriage contains romance and love, but it is a partnership based on a strong commitment of trust in each other. No matter what comes along, we will always face it together.

The call to coach involves not only the coach but the coach's family, as well. The sacrifices that are necessary to coach must be acknowledged by the spouse. The call is a call to partners who are both committed and who are seeking to make a difference in the lives of others. Without the support of a caring spouse who is equally devoted to the call, coaches will experience problems that can potentially harm the marriage. Making a difference in others begins with your family, who should always be top priority. Diane and I have enjoyed many great moments in our marriage. Some of my most beloved memories are the hugs I receive from her on the field after games, win or lose. That embrace from my wife tells me that she still believes that what we are doing together really matters. It is one of her endorsements of my efforts… It is her affirmation of our call and is priceless to me. Affirmations of love to each other are great moments in our marriage. The coach's spouse is his/her greatest asset.

One time I was watching film at the house late at night. Diane came in and looked at a few clips with me. She asked me, "Why don't you play David more at linebacker? He is good." My response was, "Diane, he is the smallest linebacker in the league. He has trouble tackling, and he is slow. But other than that, he is a good guy." She answered, "Well, I think you should play him more." I asked her, "Why should I play him more?" She answered, "Because he hugs his mother before every game." I looked at her and smiled, "I really want linebackers who tackle, not hug."

A few games later, I put David in the game, and he made three great tackles. I was amazed. After the game that night, I told my group, "You guys should hug your moms more. Show them you love 'em." The moms on the team one-by-one told me how much they appreciated me telling their sons to hug their moms and let them know you love them. Maybe Diane does not know about tackling, but she notices things I do not see. Good tackling technique is necessary in football, but so is love.

Coaches, listen to your spouse.

My two sons, Chip and Tyler, have sacrificed many holidays, weekends, family trips and family vacations because of this profession. My mother told me once that you can pick your spouse and your friends, but your children have no choice about who their parents are. Many times, I have neglected spending time with my sons because of coaching commitments. Never once have either of them complained. Taking them for granted is an easy trap to fall into because of their acceptance. Many of the family highlights we have enjoyed are games, plays, and recitals that these two guys participated in. Following my boys to their events created memories that we will always cherish. Those moments are precious.

Coach, make time for your children, and listen to them.

Priorities

Some things happen in our lives that remind us about what really matters. It is easy to fall in love with our achievements as coaches and allow our success to hypnotize us into thinking that we are doing the right thing--even though it is not true. Diane was diagnosed with cancer in 2000. The doctor explained to us that her lymphoma was incurable and that the average life span she could expect was maybe six years.

We were devastated and searched for second and third opinions. After visiting a few hospitals, the doctor at M.D. Anderson in Houston, Texas told us, "I can cure her." When he uttered that statement, we both jumped out of our chair and gave him a "bear hug." M.D. Anderson was 750 miles from our home in Georgia where her doctors arranged a specialized form of radiation unique to this tremendous cancer hospital. Her treatments began at the beginning of basketball season and lasted for three months. She received the radiation daily and had to stay near the hospital in Houston. One of my biggest regrets was that I let her go through this alone while I stayed home and coached my team. If I had to do that one over, I would have resigned as the coach and accompanied my wife through this very difficult time.

A turning point in our family's life occurred on September 9, 2001. We were home in our bed asleep when the phone rang. Diane answered and immediately burst into tears. I grabbed the phone and asked, "Who are you? What is wrong?" The nurse at the other end of this midnight phone call explained that our son Chip had been involved in an accident in Augusta, GA where he played baseball for Augusta University. I asked, "What kind of accident?" She answered, "He was ejected from his vehicle and was taken to the intensive care unit of the Medical College of Georgia." I asked, "Is he alive…? -to which she replied, "You need to get here quick."

We made the three-hour drive in the middle of the night and arrived at MCG as the sun was rising. We both bolted into the hospital praying that Chip was alive. The doctor met us with the stern caution that he was alive but in critical condition. He explained that all indications were that he was paralyzed, but the tests showed that his spine was intact, much to their surprise. We saw him lying in the bed on life support motionless. It was a horrible sight for parents and truly scared us to our very core.

We could only visit a few minutes and went to the waiting room and started praying. In a short time, the nurse came running to us and said, "Come quickly! He moved." We were overjoyed. The doctor explained to us that the next twenty-four hours would be critical to see if he survived… but at least we saw him move and eliminated paralysis. During the twelve days Chip was in the hospital, we learned that he was ejected through the driver's side windshield as his truck flipped. He traveled 60 feet through the air and landed in a pile of boulders face first. He was following a young girl on the ASU golf team home to her dorm when the accident occurred. The young lady witnessed the accident and saw Chip hurtling through the air and land in the ditch of boulders. She immediately ran to him and called 911, and as she was calling, a stranger walked up on this foggy night where the accident occurred on the "hairpin curve." The stranger knelt over Chip and began CPR. Within a few minutes, the ambulance arrived, and the stranger melted away into the fog without ever mentioning his name. To this day we do not know who he was, even though we have diligently searched to find him. It makes me believe that God sent him.

Several days later, one of the doctors confessed that when he arrived in ICU, they knew his chances were very minimal but somehow, he pulled through. He remained in the hospital for twelve days and was released to go home and recover. It was a long period of agonizing months, but he was able to walk across the stage and receive his diploma. Chip has an amazing and miraculous story of how God was not finished with him.

Mulligans

Following are the words of David Bernard Mulligan, a native of Quebec, from the 1920's:

"One day while playing in my usual foursome, I hit a ball off the first tee that was long enough but not straight. I was so provoked with myself that on impulse I stooped over and put another ball down. The other three looked at me with considerable puzzlement and one of them asked, 'What are you doing?'

'I'm taking a correction shot,' I replied.

'What do you call that?' the partner inquired.

Thinking fast, I told him that I called it a *mulligan*. After that it became kind of an unwritten rule in our foursome that you could take an extra free shot on the first tee if you were not satisfied with the original. Naturally, this always was referred to as 'taking a mulligan.'"

Thus, one legend of the origination of the "mulligan" was born, birthing the do-over shot that is still referred to as a "mulligan." Other rumors abound about how the "mulligan" came to be, but we will never know the truth, and golfers routinely make allowance for a do-over occasionally outside of competitive tournaments.

A few ironies still exist regarding Chip's accident and recovery. First, the accident occurred on Berkman's Road in Augusta a few hundred yards from Augusta National Golf Club. Second, the mysterious fellow who just walked up in the fog that night to administer CPR to Chip explained to the young lady who saw the accident, "Do not worry. He will be ok." We have searched for this man exhaustively, but never found him. He just appeared, gave CPR and vanished. Thirdly, Chip flew sixty feet through the air, the distance from the pitcher's mound to home plate. Fourthly, Chip was driving back from a bar named "Mulligan's."

God gave Chip a "Mulligan."

Coaching Burnout

The call to coach involves a strong sense of sacrificial giving, especially devoting time to other people's children. The demanding number of hours away from home are particularly difficult for the coaches' family—especially the coach's spouse. Coach burnout is a significant and growing phenomenon in the profession of coaching. Two studies regarding burnout factors shed light on the causes of undue stress in the coaching ranks. A study conducted by Ewa Herman (2020) reveals that most coaches do not suffer emotional exhaustion but rather, feel professionally undervalued. The conclusion of this study links burnout with lack of support from school leaders and a frustration with relationship efficacy. This lack of connection to players possibly stems from parental interference in the player-coach relationship.

Another revealing study by Spencer Esslinger indicates that the causes of burnout reside in a high workload, parent interference and a lack of support from school leaders. These results are very similar to the Herman research. Esslinger (2004) also posits that coaches who are more results-oriented suffer a significantly higher burnout rate than coaches whose value is placed on relationship building. While 66% of coaches admit to good relationships with parents, one-third of coaches believe that parents are a high source of stress.

My belief is that the many causes of professional burnout is a personal matter and varies with the coach and the coaching situation. Both experience and studies teach that hard work is not a source of stress, but an antidote to stress. When coaches feel they have support from their leader and a purpose in their calling, the professional demands provide a strong sense of satisfaction.

The coach whose primary goal is to win exposes herself to the stress that she views as failure. Remember the words of Dean Smith mentioned earlier, "If every game is life or death, you will die a lot." Coaches who stay in the profession for long periods are seeking a much higher standard than wins provide. The fulfillment that accompanies hard work to achieve team goals, to build lasting relationships and to create a culture of mutual trust are the ingredients that sustain coaches who desire more than winning. Pour yourself into the lives of your players, Coach! That effort will sustain you and lend a tremendous sense of satisfaction to your calling!

The Coach's Legacy

As I reflect on decades in pursuit of this coaching life, my memories are not about X's and O's or wins and losses. These memories revolve around people. When I was in grammar school, one of my favorite teachers was Mrs. Edith Sanborn. She genuinely cared for her entire class and poured herself into our lives. She was a tremendous influence on my life during a period when I was assimilating my values.

Mrs. Sanborn loved poetry and gave us an assignment to select a poem and recite it before the class. She instructed us that she would call on one student each Friday to stand before the class and recite their poem. Even though she gave us ample time to select a poem and memorize it, I failed to follow through and was not prepared when she called my name to stand before the class and recite my poem. I was horrified and had no idea what to recite. Between the time she called my name and the short walk to the front of the class, I decided to recite a funny poem that my friend James Spears had taught me.

Yellow bird, yellow bill, sitting on my windowsill.
I coaxed him in with crumbs of bread, and …
Then I knocked him in the head!

Everyone in the class laughed, except for Mrs. Sanborn. She gave me that icy glare that showed her disapproval. When school was dismissed, Mrs. Sanborn said, "Marty, please see me." Her words were, "Marty, I gave this assignment to teach you the value of poetry and help you to understand the value of words and how they influence us…but you made a mockery of the assignment. I am so disappointed in your efforts. Next Friday, I will give you a chance to redeem yourself."

I loved Mrs. Sanborn and was ashamed of my lack of effort. So… I went home and found a poem in one of my mother's poetry books. I practiced it every day anticipating my second chance. The following Friday, Mrs. Sanborn announced that "Marty will have another chance to recite a poem to the class."

Below is the poem that I chose to redeem myself. Amazingly, this poem that was memorized because of my immature prank, has personified my walk through this life. It captures the essence of my calling to coach. It was written by an anonymous author and is entitled *The Bridge Builder*.

> An old man, traveling an old highway came one evening, cold and gray
> To a chasm with banks so wide and deep that many a pilgrim feared to leap.
> The old man crossed in the twilight dim, the sullen stream held no fear for him,
> But he turned on reaching the other side and built a bridge to span the tide.
> 'Old man,' cried a pilgrim near, 'you are wasting strength in building here,
> You never again will pass this way; your journey will end at ending day.
> This bridge you have spent much labor on will serve not you when the task is done,

You have crossed the chasm deep and wide; why build this
bridge to span the tide?'
But the builder raised his old gray head, 'Good friend, in the
path I came,' he said,
There follows, after me today a youth whose feet must pass
this way.
He too must cross in the twilight dim,
Good friend, I built this bridge for him.'

When I finished reciting the poem, the class was hushed, and Mrs. Sanborn was staring at me with tears in her eyes. She told me, "Marty, I want to see you when the bell rings." To my amazement, she hugged me and said, "I am so proud of you. I knew you could do it. That poem could very well turn out to be the story of your life." She was right.

Coaching is bridge building for others.

REFERENCES

Bush, G.W. (2018). *A Father's Impact on Child Development.* Children's Bureau. Retrieved From all4kids.org.

Buss, Sarah. (2020). *Radical Humility: Essays on Ordinary Acts of Humility*, Belt Publishing,

Child and Family Research. (2022). Retrieved from https://child and family research.utexas.

Cook, Andy. (2017). *The Myth of the Fatherless Society.* The Conversation. Retrieved from the Conversation.com.

Ehrmann, Joe. (2004) *Season of Life.* Published by Simon & Schuster, New York, New York.

Ellis, Lyman. (2020). *Do Coaches Who are Servant Leaders Promote Virtue in Their Athletes?*

Esslinger, Spencer. (2004). St. Cloud State University Press. *Burnout Factors of High School Basketball Coaches.* Retrieved https://repository.stcloudstate.edu/pess_etds.

Evans, Martin. (1970). *The Effects of Supervisory Behavior on the Path-Goal Relationship.* Organizational Behavior and Human Performance, 5/3)

Fathers.com (2022). *The Consequences of Fatherlessness.*

Frenette, Gene. (2021). *Unbearable.* Florida Times Union.

Gallimore, Ronald and Roland Tharp. (1975). *Reflections and Reanalysis of John Wooden's Teaching Practices.* The Sport Psychologist.

Herman, Ewa. (2020). International Journal of Sports Science and Coaching. *What makes Coaches Burn Out on Their Job? Prevalence of Correlates of Coaches' Burnout.*

House, Robert J. (1971). *A Path-Goal Theory of Leader Effectiveness.* Administration Science Quarterly, 16/3.

Journal of Character Education, Number 6, Volume 1, pp.1-12. Retrieved July 18, 2022 from: https://www.infoagepub.com/jrce-issue.html?i=p5e65061367c85.

Keegan, Richard J., Chris Harwood, Christopher Spray and David Lavallee. (2009). Psychology of Sport and Exercise. *A Qualitative Investigation Exploring the Motivational Climate in Early Career Sports Participants.*

Knight, Bobby. (2016). Sports and Fitness. *Coaches serving as Father Figures Should be Role Models.*

Li, Sitan and Juan Li. (2021). *Fostering Trust: Authoritarian, Benevolent, and Moral Paternalistic Leadership Styles and the Coach–Athlete Relationship.* Social, Behavior and Personality-Journal. Volume 49, Number 12, 2021, pp. 1-11(11)

Mastro, Victor and Johnny Shevalla. (1996) The Coffin Corner, 18/5. Retrieved from Profootballresearchers.org.

Powers, Chris. (2020) Golf Digest. *Did You Know: Where Did the Term Mulligan Originate?* April 1, 2020.

Robinson, G. M., and Marshall Magnusen. (2022). *Servant Leadership, Leader Effectiveness, and the Role of Political Skill: A Study of Interscholastic Sport Administrators and Coaches.* Baylor University Department of Exercise Science and Sport Management.

APPENDICES

Appendix A – John Wooden's Pyramid of Success

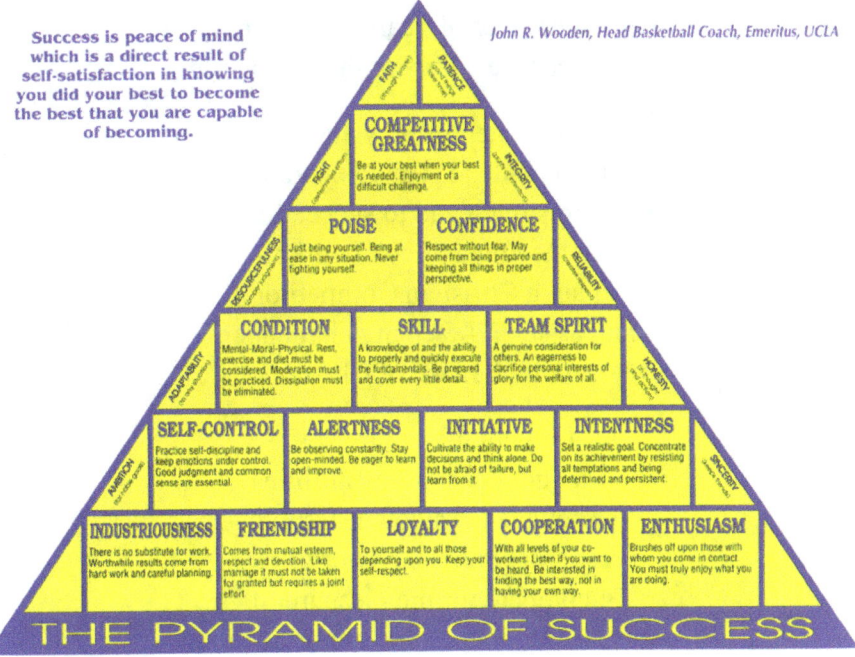

Appendix B – FCA Competitor's Creed

The Competitor's Creed

I am a Christian first and last.
I am created in the likeness of
God Almighty to bring Him glory.
I am a member of Team Jesus Christ.
I wear the colors of the cross.

I am a Competitor now and forever.
I am made to strive, to strain,
to stretch and to succeed
in the arena of competition.
I am a Christian Competitor
and as such, I face my challenger
with the face of Christ.

I do not trust in myself.
I do not boast in my abilities
or believe in my own strength.
I rely solely on the power of God.
I compete for the pleasure of
my Heavenly Father, the honor of Christ
and the reputation of the Holy Spirit.

My attitude on and off
the field is above reproach –
my conduct beyond criticism.
Whether I am preparing,
practicing or playing;
I submit to God's authority
and those He has put over me.

I respect my coaches, officials,
teammates and competitors
out of respect for the Lord.

My body is the temple of Jesus Christ.
I protect it from within and without.
Nothing enters my body that
does not honor the Living God.
My sweat is an offering to my Master.
My soreness is a sacrifice to my Savior.

I give my all – all of the time.
I do not give up. I do not give in.
I do not give out. I am the Lord's warrior –
a competitor by conviction
and a disciple of determination.
I am confident beyond reason
because my confidence lies in Christ.
The results of my efforts
must result in His glory.

ABOUT THE AUTHOR

Dr. Marty Durden is a career coach who has achieved a unique standing in the coaching profession by having teams win multiple state championships in four different sports. Durden's teams have captured state championships in basketball (1980), baseball (1995), golf (2010-2011, 2021), and football (1983, 1987, 1988, 1989, 2020) over the span of five decades.

Durden's expertise is in the field of servant leadership coaching. He is considered an expert in researching the motivational aspects of servant-leadership coaching, having sampled 3,000+ student-athletes and coaches to identify the innate value of servant-leadership in athletics. This study is the only one of its kind in existence.

His research has identified the inherent motivational aspects of servant-leadership coaching and reveals the transformational influence this philosophy possesses, especially on generation Z student-athletes. He has written and researched this topic extensively, espousing the philosophy of "A Higher Standard than Winning" that emphasizes effort, teamwork, and improvement above results.

He teaches that success is the result of concentrated effort that precedes athletic accomplishments. Dr. Durden's research shows us the powerful influence of servant-leadership coaching and that this philosophy effectively motivates the modern athlete. His research affirms the effectiveness of servant-leadership coaching, and he believes that coaches who lead as servants have tremendous cultural influence on young people preparing them to be good parents, spouses, and more productive citizens.

With 48 years of successful experience in sports leadership, Coach Durden has most recently served as the Athletic Director at Calvary Christian School in Columbus, GA. He is also an adjunct professor of Sport Leadership at Belhaven University, Concordia Texas University and Houston Christian University and shares his insights as a writer and practitioner.

Durden is a lifelong advocate of the Fellowship of Christian Athletes and has taught Sunday school to young people for 30 plus years. He founded the West Central Georgia FCA Chapter and has hosted numerous FCA ministry events.

Marty is married to Diane. They have two sons: Chip, a baseball and football coach, and Tyler is a computer engineer in Decatur, GA and married to Emily, a high school Algebra teacher.

Having enjoyed a long and successful career in athletics, Dr. Durden is poised to deepen his teaching of sports management and has founded a non-profit organization named *A Higher Standard of Leadership*. His experience as both a practitioner and theorist have prepared him to mentor aspiring sport leaders. He is available to assist athletic programs, corporations, churches, faith-based schools, and businesses as they build the cultural blueprint of their sports programs.

www.ingramcontent.com/pod-product-compliance
Lightning Source LLC
LaVergne TN
LVHW022325080426
835508LV00013BA/1316

9 7 9 8 9 8 7 4 3 1 2 0 7